YOUR SECRET AMBITIONS DON'T HAVE TO WAIT

"My family couldn't afford to give me lessons. I dreamt of fulfilling this wish for thirty years and finally started lessons. This is the only thing I do for *me.*"

—Gail Clifford, a late learner

"It's an explosion! Adults are searching for something that challenges them intellectually and feeds them spiritually. It challenges the mind, soul and ears."

—Alison Barr, national chairwoman of the Independent Music Teachers Forum

"When things get hectic at work, I close my door, roll the chair to the keyboard on my right and play away."

—Samuel Andrews, New York businessman

IF THEY CAN DO IT, SO CAN YOU!

WHEN I SIT DOWN TO PLAY

*A Guide to
Fulfilling Your Dream
of Playing the Piano
and Keyboard*

Joan St. James

KENSINGTON BOOKS
http://www.kensingtonbooks.com

Piano diagram appearing in Chapter 5 used with permission from: Baldwin Piano and Organ Company, Mason, Ohio 45040-5301

Musical works appearing in Chapter 7 used with permission from: Alfred Publishing Co., Inc., Van Nuys, California 91410-0003

KENSINGTON BOOKS are published by

Kensington Publishing Corp.
850 Third Avenue
New York, NY 10022

ISBN 1-57566-619-7

Kensington and the K logo Reg. U.S. Pat. & TM Off.

First Kensington Printing: November, 2000
10 9 8 7 6 5 4 3 2 1

Printed in the United States of America

To my parents, whose unconditional love, support and sacrifice made it possible for me to pursue a musical career.

To the late Norman Weiser, whose original concept and guiding hand led me to write this book, my eternal gratitude.

ACKNOWLEDGMENTS

This book could not have been written without the help of these people who gave of their time, effort and patience. For their enduring support, friendship and love, my thanks to Dolores Janes; Al Zoller; Doug Larson; George and Jeri Sape, Esq.; Brian Platton, Esq.; Mark Hunter; E. L. Lancaster; Jason Weber and Guy Kettlehack.

To Jeanne Scova, who spent countless, tedious hours at the computer typing and editing this book, I couldn't have done it without you. Our long friendship was tested and we survived.

My sincere gratitude to Walter Zacharius for making the publication of this book a reality.

To my special friend and fellow pianist, Michael, my heartfelt thanks for being the selfless, caring person you are. Many roadblocks were lifted because of your eagerness to help, your considerable knowledge, and your unswerving loyalty.

CONTENTS

You Can Do It

You find yourself singing in the shower, and suddenly you imagine yourself playing that song on the piano. Your fingers tap against the bathroom tiles as they might on the keyboard. You dream and find yourself seated at a baby grand, the life of the party, playing away into the night. Fantasy takes over, and you are seated at a gleaming Steinway on the great stage of Carnegie Hall with the New York Philharmonic as the background. You're playing the Rachmaninoff Second Piano Concerto and finish to thunderous applause. You have been transported into a world of fantasy when reality hits like a bolt of lightning. All comes crashing down when you realize it's just that—pure fantasy. Even the memory of the songs you actually *did* once play on the piano seems foolish. There's no way you could do *that* again. It's been too long. You've forgotten too much. There's no way you could get back even the little you knew.

Maybe you've *never* played the piano, but have always dreamed of playing. Music has stirred you like nothing else. What must it be like simply to sit down at a piano and *play*—to summon up those wonderful sounds yourself? What would it be like to write a song—to write the lyrics for it, to arrange it as Nelson Riddle and Don Costa did for Frank Sinatra and Rosemary Clooney?

You finally throw in the towel and succumb to the fact it will never be, and your dream vanishes.

How wrong you are! Whether you've never played before or want to resume lessons after being away from music for a long time, *you can do it!* You *can* play those songs you hear on tape and subconsciously finger on the table. Those lost years of not practicing are not entirely lost. As long as music is your passion and you have the desire to learn to play or get back to playing, there's more than hope. Playing in public is not as far-fetched as you think either. All you have to do is give yourself a chance. Stick with it and there's no telling how far you can go.

I am amazed at the number of people who go through life never fulfilling their dreams because "it's too late." That is sheer nonsense. Okay, some dreams may be unrealistic. It's probably true you can't become a prima ballerina or play shortstop for the New York Yankees starting at age 45 or 50. But with piano, there is no age limit for beginners.

As a student at the Juilliard School in New York, I, like many of my colleagues, had to work my way through school. Taking on piano students was the most viable way of doing that. Many of those students were professional people with comfortable careers. Some were past retirement age. Now with success in their corner plus leisure time, they were ready to "work" in order to "play."

One student was a prominent local surgeon who played by ear, but only in the key of E-flat. His motive for taking lessons was to learn how to play in other keys. "I never had the time for anything but studying once I entered medical school. I then got married and had a thriving career. Now that I'm about to retire, I'm not going to let this chance go by. I may never play like Arthur Rubinstein, but that doesn't mean I can't enjoy *playing* as much as Rubinstein did. . . ."

Teaching this doctor about keys other than E-flat meant teaching him the rudiments of music theory and chord structure as well as technique. It wasn't easy; his patience threshold was very low. He wanted to arrive at his goal by "yesterday." He did stick with it, though, and was eventually able to display his newfound skill at every party he went to where there was a piano.

Another student who had prior training actually developed deformed fingers from a combination of faulty technical training and exceptionally long fingernails. She was convinced she'd never play again. Once she trimmed those nails and was given heavy doses of technical exercises and scales, she began to respond. She actually played better at 45 than she ever had at 15.

My most heartfelt experience was listening to a 70-year-old grandmother burble like a child as she told me about taking piano lessons for the first time. She showed me how she could play a tune with both hands on the keyboard. It was her lifelong dream. To quote New York Yankee great Yogi Berra: "It's not over 'til it's over."

I am constantly amazed by the number of people, some well-known, who have harbored that same dream. Some forged ahead and did something about it while others continued to dream on. Take for instance:

Regis Philbin of *Live with Regis and Kathie Lee* started piano lessons in 1988 and periodically plays for his TV audience. He tries to practice five days weekly—half an hour each day. Regis spends a lot of time on scales and chords and claims to have discouraging moments, but he keeps at it. He's had letters pour in from viewers saying how much he has inspired them to begin lessons.

Fay Wray of *King Kong* fame: "I always wanted to play and started lessons late in life. I'll never regret it."

Hugh Carey, former New York governor, recently told me he's currently taking piano lessons as are many of his friends and peers. He loves to sing and will probably learn to play well enough to be able to accompany himself.

Menahem Pressler, a concert pianist, finally made his debut at Carnegie Hall in February 1996 at age 72. He continues with a heavy schedule as both soloist and ensemble player.

Noah Adams, who is host of National Public Radio's nightly program, *All Things Considered,* and author of *Piano Lessons: Music, Love and True Adventures* (Delacorte Press) questions his befuddlement as to why at 51 he would suddenly spend $11,500 for a Steinway he neither knows how to play nor has the time to practice. He started with a computer program, then moved on to a sight-reading system on tapes and a 10-day adult course at a night school. He took lessons as a child but admitted: "I'd rather be outside and play football." As an adult, he awakens at 6:00 A.M. daily and does nothing before getting in an hour's worth of practice. Adams says there are advantages to a late start. As an adult, "You have so much Western music in your system that you know what the song sounds like. When I play a wrong note, I know it. A child will just keep on playing." Taking formal lessons with a teacher twice a week, he says, "There's nothing I do in a day when I wouldn't rather be at a piano."

Father Willman, my childhood parish priest, spent most of his free time learning to play. He used to stop by my parents' home to play duets with me.

An excerpt from a letter by a convalescent home resident to Steinway and Sons in New York: "Enclosed is a copy of the article highlighting my musical experience and other background information prior to my first recital. I am planning another recital on or before next fall. I hope the enclosed article plus my drive and determination will be an inspiration to many individuals who would like to play the piano and feel they are too old to learn."

A Late Learner reports: "My family couldn't afford to give me lessons. I dreamt of fulfilling this wish for 30 years and finally started lessons. This is the only thing I do for *me.*"

Mickey Mantle—the late Yankee legend used to sit on the piano bench with me and watch me play. He loved music and often expressed his desire to learn.

Billy Martin—another late Yankee legend and Mickey's good friend had a wonderful musical ear and a good voice. He surprised me one night by joining me as I sang a few Japanese songs in the native tongue for some Japanese guests in the audience. He said he learned those songs while in the service.

Phil Donahue—talk show host; *Bruce Jenner*—Olympic swimming champ.

My list is endless and continues to grow. Today, when I perform at social functions, it's the norm to have guests reveal their secret ambition. One man, the owner of a prosperous New York business, described how he contacted a local music school for a teacher and now practices both at home and on his digital keyboard at the office. "When things get hectic at work, I close my door, roll the chair to the keyboard on my right and play away." Another gathering of thirty people exposed more music lovers. *Three* men out of that group were taking lessons.

So you see, you're not alone in your quest to learn. You undoubtedly have your own names to add to a never-ending list.

Alison Barr, National Chairwoman of the Independent Music Teachers Forum, says: "It's an explosion! Adults are searching for something that challenges them intellectually and feeds them spiritually. It challenges the mind, soul and ears."

Maria Eftimiades, in a *New York Times* article, states that more adults are sitting down to scales and sonatas, sometimes vying with their own children for practice time. Nationwide, teachers are reviewing their teaching methods, long geared toward children, to accommodate the adult. It's now easy to learn classical pieces, big-band tunes, Beatle songs, etc. She goes on to say that many musical organizations are exploring ways to handle this sudden surge. Their national convention seminars and workshops offer tips on handling adult students. The advice ranges from evening/weekend classes—group lessons allowing adults to socialize—organizing trips to concerts, and arranging adult-only recitals.

The National Piano Foundation produced three videos geared toward adults returning to lessons and to teachers who had never taught adults. Their slide presentation, "Teaching *Bigger* Fingers to Play," is a take-off on John Thompson's perennial classic for beginners, *Teaching Little Fingers to Play.* Their current project focuses on children and parents playing together.

Van Cliburn, a classmate of mine at the Juilliard School, had a profound thought: "Piano is one of the few constants in the world. It is reliable—never changes."

There are a handful of reasons why adults are flocking to what has become the biggest emerging market today. Taking piano lessons has been proven not only to combat stress and encourage creativity, but also to open doors to social opportunities. It also encourages children to want to learn when they see their parents learning. In actuality, learning to play the piano is a *craft* just like learning to ski, to play golf or tennis. There are myths falsely claiming that you *must* have a good ear to play, you *must* have long fingers to expand beyond an octave, only the *young* can learn! While these claims have some merit, these attributes are a *plus*—not a *must!* Anyone brought into the world with a musical talent has a special gift from God. It gives that person the distinct advantage of having "one foot in the door." Yet even with that gift, you will need to be shown how to bring out that talent and how to refine it. To put it simply: gift or no gift—*You Can Do It.*

I am convinced that one of the greatest gifts given to us is music itself. It affects each and every one of us in a unique way. Listen to some words from Thomas Moore's recent CD, "Music for the Soul" (Harper Perennial): "Use this music . . . meditate to it, sit with it and hear it with a friend . . . solid food for the soul." If there's any tension built up within you, music slowly dissolves it and opens the way to peace and harmony.

The May 1997 article from the *Juilliard Journal* by pianist/ composer Marvin Hamlish says that his short stint as a teacher saw arts education help young children feel good about themselves and their accomplishments. "When they played a new song or recited new lines, I saw their self-esteem grow." The article continues with a survey by psychologist Frances Rauscher from the University of California at Irvine. She observed that preschoolers who met twice weekly developed music skills that enabled them to not only sing together on pitch and in rhythm but improve their mathematical skills as well. Students involved in a music program outperformed the non-music group every time, according to recent college entrance examination board data. This is a major plus for high school students taking the SAT test. Reports reveal that they scored a full 61 points higher on the verbal portion and 46 points higher on the math. Rauscher's article, "Music and the Mind," also quotes a statement made by New York City's first lady, Donna Hanover Giuliani, in her newspaper article "Cool Schools: With a Song in Their Hearts." It's regarding progressive music programs in New York City public schools that highlight the power of music on a child's overall sociological development. While only touching the intellectual effects of music education, the article states that recent research has established an unmistakable causal link between music and spatial intelligence.

Music has long been recognized for its healing power, both physically and mentally. It's now considered a basic necessity. Confirming this is an article entitled "Learning Improved by Arts Training" from *Nature*, a world-renowned scientific publication: "Training in music and art can help children improve basic reading, writing and arithmetic skills."

The President's Committee on the Arts and Humanities finds: "Safe havens of music, theater, dance and visual arts programs have proved particularly potent in stemming violence and drug abuse and in keeping students from dropping out of school." There are numerous articles confirming a significant correlation between arts education and improved academic performance and student attendance.

From these few articles, you can see the enormous benefit that music has on the young. In actuality, it benefits *everyone!* Studies have shown that an adult taking music lessons becomes less dependent on nicotine and alcohol because he or she is now involved in a time-consuming project. Boredom is just about alleviated. Isn't that one of the reasons one becomes dependent on these substances anyway? If you're from the school of "can't teach an old dog new tricks," explain how Picasso experimented with a new style of painting in his nineties. How Verdi was able to compose new operas in his eighties or George Bernard Shaw write new plays in his nineties? In addition to the famous artists, in an article by Gene D. Cohen, M.D., Director of the Center on Aging, Health and Humanities at George Washington University in Washington, D.C., he cited a folk-art painter who didn't pick up a paintbrush until he was 85 years old . . . an 81-year-old whose life changed when she discovered literature . . . a man who began to sculpt in his mid-60s and had a solo exhibit at New York's Museum of Modern Art . . . a woman who started painting as a hobby at 56 and covered the museum walls across the country when in her 70s. He concluded by saying that, scientifically, the brain responds to stimulation and challenges by the cells sprouting new extensions, therefore improving communication. Brain cells respond to mental exercise just as muscle cells respond to physical exercise. In other words, "Use it or lose it."

Learning to play the piano *can* start at any age, and once you learn how to play and see your skills steadily improving so that you're comfortable with your playing, all kinds of doors can swing open for you. Once those doors open, are you aware of how far you can go and the many ways a piano can be used? Here are just some of the opportunities to look forward to:

AT HOME

- Play for relaxation and pleasure
- Play for family
- Play for friends and guests
- Teach children and grandchildren
- Teach other adults
- Play for sing-along sessions
- Volunteer as pianist for at-home functions
- Play at birthday parties for children
- Play piano duets and piano duos (if second piano is available)
- Play for children at a day-care center
- Play for in-home civic meetings
- Accompany vocalists and instrumentalists

VOLUNTEER

- Nursing homes
- Adult homes
- Children's wards in hospitals
- Day-care centers
- AIDS hospices
- Veterans' hospitals
- Church functions
- Prisons
- Civic clubs like Elks, Moose, Kiwanis

JOB OPPORTUNITIES

- Prisons through government grants
- Pianist for church choir, weddings, funerals
- Teach piano to both children and adults
- Vocal or instrumental accompanist
- Play for auditions
- Background music at banks and stores
- Salesperson at a piano/keyboard store

AS YOU PROGRESS

- Piano bars
- Cocktail lounges
- Dining rooms
- Restaurants
- Private parties
- Cruises
- Bank lobbies
- Cabarets
- Jazz clubs
- Theaters
- Concerts
- Recitals

If you re-read that list and let your imagination run wild, the fact that a musical career may be in the cards for you seems unimaginable at this point. Yet—why not? When I started playing the piano at age three and a half, I had no idea my destiny was music. I pursued it, and by the time I reached age 16, I was the featured artist on a weekly radio program on Long Island, New York. I taught piano to youngsters and adults throughout my high school years and continued until graduation from the Juilliard School in New York. After a few years of solo playing, I formed an instrumental trio and was playing an engagement in New York when discovered by bandleader Guy Lombardo. He invited the trio to appear opposite his Royal Canadians and participate in programs with bandleaders Count Basie and Duke Ellington. I went on to organize an all-girl trio at the suggestion of Lombardo. The instrumental combination was piano, bass, and drums, but we never anticipated singing three-part harmony. That came about accidentally, and before long I was arranging music for us both instrumentally and vocally. I started to write my own music and then added lyrics to it. This eventually led to TV and radio appearances and recordings. A sketch of my career just proves it *can* be done. If it happened for me, why not for you? With perseverance and determination, there is no telling where you can go.

2

Therapeutic Benefits Through Music

Nature and medicine's greatest accomplice is without a doubt music therapy. That's a powerful statement, yet almost daily new evidence appears to back this up. I saw this with my own eyes when I started doing volunteer work in a New York nursing home. Once a week I played the piano and sang for the residents and got them involved in the music. Weary faces lit up when familiar songs were played. They were recalling precious moments and key players in their lives. Pent-up emotions were triggered, and this release started them singing. I saw serious stroke patients unable to speak suddenly sing a song that was familiar to them. Immobile patients responded to rhythmic tunes by clapping hands and tapping their feet.

When the director of entertainment saw this, she alerted the medical staff. They started appearing at the door and watched in awe as more and more residents took part. Every session added newcomers. As I got to know the residents on an individual basis, the message was always the same. They expressed how much they looked forward to the entertainment. Most said that while the music eased both their burden and their boredom, the greatest benefit was the therapy each and every one derived on a personal level.

Matthew H.M. Lee, M.D., M.P.H., professor and acting chairman of the Rusk Institute of Rehabilitation in New York, verified what I saw. In his various articles, he wrote: "The concept of preventive medicine through music therapy is an emerging market about to explode . . . music therapy could save medicare millions of dollars as a replacement for drugs and other costly therapies if used in rehabilitation treatment of chronic illness and prevention . . . music therapy has been an invaluable tool with many of our rehabilitation patients. There is no question that the relationship of music and medicine will blossom because of the advent of previously unavailable techniques that can now show the effects of music."

Dr. Lee gave me a video that he edited from his book *Rehabilitation, Music and Well-Being*. Watching this video and seeing how music helped the severely disabled at Goldwater Memorial Hospital in New York was exhilarating and inspirational. Goldwater has a music therapy center for the severely disabled in conjunction with the Department of Music of New York University. The tape shows that music and the arts can improve the rehabilitation of individuals in the area of mental functioning, breathing capacity, pain, socialization, vocational skills, and self-expression. It points out that scientific medicine is recognizing the validity of music therapy to healing. It also has power to affect the areas of chronic pain in the human body.

Dr. Norman Vincent Peale, a personal friend of Dr. Lee, "watched with admiration his growing expertise in the area of pain, its understanding and treatment. The use of music therapy to measure and control pain reactions gives new dimensions of hope and will be a milestone in the art and science of healing." Kitty Carlisle Hart, Chairman of the New York State Council on the Arts, said she was always convinced of the tremendous therapeutic effect of music: "While music has always played an integral part in people's lives in the world's cultures, the marriage of music and medicine will, no doubt, create further support for the use of music as a major therapeutic modality."

Two noted experts corroborate Dr. Lee's findings. One is Oliver Sachs, M.D., Professor of Neurology at Albert Einstein College of Medicine in New York. He said, "I regard music therapy as a tool of great power in many neurological disorders—Parkinson's and Alzheimer's—because of its unique capacity to organize or reorganize cerebral function when it has been damaged."

Karl H. Pribram, M.D., Ph.D., Professor Emeritus, Stanford University; The James P. and Anna King Distinguished Professor, Radford University; Eminent Scholar, Commonwealth of Virginia, finds, "Music is one of the most profound human achievements. It complements human linguistic ability and enters deeply into the human emotional experience. As such, it is a tremendous contribution to healing when used by trained professionals."

A recent article in the Sunday's *New York Times Magazine* showed an inmate in his cell at the Jackson Correctional Institution in Black River Falls, Wisconsin. On his bunk bed was a digital keyboard. This inmate, who is serving time for armed robbery and attempted homicide, states, "I'm here for my crime. You've got to make the best of it. This is where I spend my quality time. I'm a paralegal and I do a lot of studies, play my keyboard in my room and things like that. I don't have anything to hide."

How fortunate he is to have the intelligence to make the most of an unfortunate experience. Music is not only assisting him in filling those long, lonely hours, it's a positive step in helping him reorganize his priorities and reevaluate the true meaning of life.

Another believer in the power of music is Dr. Mel Richardson, surgeon and medical director and chief-of-staff at a major hospital in the Midwest. He said, "Studies have actually shown that surgery goes better when music is played in the operating room."

MUSIC AS THERAPY

While all this knowledge is an amazing and miraculous break-through for those less fortunate, without the therapists to ad-minister and supervise the treatment, all is lost. Dr. Fadi Joseph Bejjani, Ph.D., research professor and Director, Human Per-formance Analysis Laboratory, New York University; President, MEDART U.S.A., recognized their significance: "Having worked extensively with music therapists for the last few years, I have learned to appreciate their professionalism, research, and clini-cal abilities. I strongly believe that they should have a promi-nent role in health care delivery." In a brochure put out by the National Association for Music Therapy, Inc., in Silver Spring, Maryland, the functions of a therapist and its objectives are clearly outlined. A therapist assesses emotional well-being, physical health, social functioning, communication abilities, and cognitive skills through musical responses. Once the client is evaluated, a recommendation is made for either individual or group sessions based on client needs. Some of the topics cov-ered in these sessions are improvisation, music listening and learning, song writing, lyric discussion, imagery, and perfor-mance.

There are many facilities throughout the world that employ accredited therapists. As with any professional specializing in human needs, a music therapist must complete an approved music therapy program from one of seventy undergraduate or graduate colleges and universities. Internship and board certifi-cation follow. In the northeast corridor of the United States, there are three programs in Pennsylvania alone that have excel-lent credentials—Hahnemann University and Temple University in Philadelphia and Immaculata College in Immaculata. Cam-bridge, Massachusetts, has Lesley College Graduate School while New York has programs at New York University in the city and Molloy College in Rockville Centre, Long Island. Musically, to qualify, one must be accomplished in piano, voice, and guitar.

A knowledge of composition, theory, history, improvisation, arranging, and conducting is recommended. Being able to sight-read and transpose at sight is an added plus as is the ability to dance in order to demonstrate expressive movements to music. Clinically, to put all of this to use, one must understand different cultures, their unique needs and problems.

All this comprehensive study and background is essential so that a certified music therapist can work in a wide variety of settings. Music therapists serve clients of all ages in medical and psychiatric hospitals addressing the problems of the emotionally disturbed, the mentally and physically handicapped, the learning disabled, and those with psychiatric and neurological disorders. The need to assist patients with physical and terminal illnesses in such geriatric facilities as nursing homes and senior centers is enormous. Add rehabilitative and correctional facilities; drug, alcohol, and hospice programs; day care and mental health centers; plus out-patient clinics, schools and private practice—it's enough to boggle the mind. Did you know that a certified music therapist can also assist in stress reduction, childbirth, and biofeedback? Indeed, music is a major component in altering the lives of those both with and without afflictions.

The benefits of the work performed by a music therapist is continually being substantiated by the results. When feelings are released and self-esteem is elevated—when frustration is eased and agitation and irritability are reduced—a patient can only benefit. It's been proven that music triggers short- and long-term memory as well as improving cognitive motor and daily living skills. We know how it distracts from pain through relaxation. The quality of life can only get better when one's dignity is restored and motivation is aroused. This is when the desire for socializing and communication can be seen. Self-expression is finally back because of the positive change in physical, behavioral and emotional disorders.

On an individual basis, those with less severe ailments like carpal tunnel syndrome, tendinitis, mild forms of arthritis, and physical injuries can find the solution through different methods. Rest is foremost in any healing process, with exercise and medical treatment running a close parallel. Teamwork is important in curing ailments. If a problem is inflammatory in nature, rest is advocated and anti-inflammatory drugs are prescribed. This worked for me when I had a mild case of tendinitis in my left thumb. My problem was brought on by overuse of the wrist muscles. I persevered and somehow managed to play nightly with a splint supporting my thumb. Being under contract and not wanting to cancel my engagement, I eased up on my left hand to facilitate healing. There were moments when I thought I'd have to throw in the towel because of excruciating pain, but I made it. With a more severe case of tendinitis, I would have been sidelined.

I gained new admiration for Byron Janis, a student of Vladimir Horowitz and one of the world's great piano virtuosos, when I read his tale of woe. After a series of incidents that included the loss of the tendon and numbness to the little finger of the left hand after running through a glass door and an auto accident that caused neck problems and severe bursitis in the right shoulder, he succumbed to crippling psoriatic arthritis at age 45. He and his wife, Maria, daughter of screen legend Gary Cooper, kept this a guarded secret for many years.

Despite the pain and limitations brought on by this disease, Janis continued to concertize. His wrists and fingers would swell, causing intense pain while practicing, yet on stage he was transformed, and his playing seemed effortless. As the disease progressed, he became moody, nervous, and depressed and thought his playing days were over. He took cortisone, pain killers, tranquilizers, and anti-inflammatory drugs, and still his fingers wouldn't respond. Fear took over, and in 1984 he stopped playing.

Janis began to take stock and eventually became aware of the fact that he had created his own prison. Realizing that fear breeds fear, he took the attitude that "while I can't control the arthritis, I can control how I cope with it. . . ." As he became less stressful, things improved immensely.

Miraculous things happened once he revealed his secret of arthritis to the world. He opened up, relaxed, and accepted these major factors in reducing stress and inducing health. Janis developed a very personal relationship with God and adopted the motto, "Let go and let God."

"My music shows my feelings about life," he said. "I still have arthritis, but it doesn't have me." While acknowledging that medical treatment is essential, he advocates listening to your body. Prayer is important, as is belief, in healing. He claims he conquered the disease largely through his beliefs and through the help of his friend, Israeli psychic Uri Geller.

Throughout this debilitating disease, Janis remained strong and is now playing again. In his latest venture, Janis is offering a concert debut of his new Broadway musical based on Victor Hugo's "The Hunchback of Notre Dame." He wrote the music, and Hal Hackady wrote the lyrics. His statement, and I quote— "if I can do it, so can you"—is one we should all adhere to.

Concert pianists Gary Graffman and Leon Fleischer, both colleagues of Byron Janis, encountered problems, too, but of a different nature. Their malady was a performance-related dysfunction that affected the right hand only. Graffman had no pain, no numbness, no tingling, but in playing octaves, the fourth finger continually drew in, dragging the fifth finger in with it. Leon Fleischer's problems arose in part because of the mechanics of playing. After numerous inaccurate medical reports, he found that work-related problems—in his case inflamed tendons and nerve compression—hampers not only pianists, but instrumentalists in general.

It's easy to see how a violinist can suffer from neck, shoulder, and arm pain. The abnormal position maintained in order to grip the violin and the bow is extremely stressful to the upper part of the body. Harpists have to be careful so as not to cramp their hands. Flutists must check for skin eruptions on the mouth and chin. Trumpet players develop outpouching of the upper airway because of the strain of hitting high notes. Cellists don't escape either. They encounter back strain due to their rigid sitting position while playing. Instrumentalists have to be wary of potential trouble, but they are not alone. Dancers who overwork can develop strained or torn ligaments in the feet and legs. Singers and actors are acutely aware of how delicate the throat is.

So there we have it for the pluses and minuses of having a career in the arts.

The biggest culprit that confronts people of all ages and to varying degrees is arthritis. Whether one has it or not, "It must be my arthritis" is a common cliché. Basically, arthritis is an inflammation that causes aches and pains to the joints and connective tissue in the body. The more severe cases add heat, stiffness, and swelling to the existing aches and pains. Osteoarthritis is a degenerative wear-and-tear disease of the joints that comes with aging. It is milder and less inflammatory than rheumatoid arthritis and does not affect the entire body. Rheumatoid, on the other hand, is a crippling disease that often causes progressive damage to tissues and has the potential of debilitating the entire body.

Both forms of arthritis require care to ward off further damage. The mild form is treated with medication, such as aspirin, rest, exercise, heat, and vitamins like niacin. Water exercise is especially good for the body as a whole. If you have a pool or have access to one, the resistance caused by pushing gently against the water is highly beneficial to arthritis sufferers. The hands and wrists profit immeasurably by underwater movements such as opening and closing the palm, stretching the fingers, rotating the wrists, and clenching the fists.

Playing the piano is equally beneficial. At the same time that it alleviates stiffness, it strengthens both wrists and fingers. It can prevent arthritis from deforming the fingers and alter deformities already there. Stamina and flexibility increase naturally regardless of the type of exercise. As always, rest is "numero uno." As you resume playing, use common sense.

The medical profession has made great strides in recognizing and treating the specific physical problems and symptoms of career artists. The scope of the practice is rivaling that of sports medicine. Doctors and therapists are acutely aware of how easy it is to overuse and strain the muscle-tendon unit, inducing carpal tunnel syndrome and tendinitis. Any repetitive motion of the flexor muscle gives out warning signals ahead of time through numbness and a tingling sensation. One often gets relief by shaking the hands and moving the fingers, but be cautious. If pain persists, there is help available.

Major cities in the United States like Boston, Chicago, Cleveland, New York, Philadelphia and San Francisco have performing arts clinics. They are thriving and continue to grow and mature. There is individualized treatment available for neuromuscular disorders caused by over-practice and grueling concert schedules. Many times a deep massage is all that's needed to relieve over-worked, stressed-out bodies. I relied on massage as well as chiropractic to "straighten out the kinks" and re-align my body. It was the ultrasonic sound treatment my chiropractor used on my right shoulder that erased a mean case of bursitis. Though I've never had it, acupuncture is another alternative. These treatments can be found both inside and outside clinics. A medical journal specifically for musicians called *The Medical Problems of Musicians* constantly updates information, techniques, and therapies and can be found in the reference section of most performing arts libraries.

If you haven't taken up the piano because you have an affliction, you now know there is help out there for you. There is more benefit to be gained by starting than not. It's also important to remember that you want to have fun. You're not out to compete with the pros. Whether your career is prospering or you're happily retired, it's now time to take care of *you*.

Improvement is automatic as one progresses and expands. It can be done. I know this from my experience as a teacher. All that is needed is the desire, time, and lots of patience. I know how easy it is to become discouraged and consider throwing in the towel. It was due to constant reassurance and inspiration from people crossing my path that I hung in and went on to a most rewarding career. Now it's my turn to pass this motivation along.

3

Good Teachers: Why They're Important and How to Find One

Throughout our school years, we are exposed to teachers who run the gamut from very good to really bad. We joke about this as we grade them on a scale from one to ten. Teachers in the music profession are by no means exempt. Just because someone plays the piano brilliantly doesn't automatically qualify him or her as a good teacher. My second piano teacher was a good example of this. We literally played the piano for each other until his wife alerted my parents that he wasn't teaching me anything. (The woman who came to me for lessons with deformed fingers after years of incompetent training is another unfortunate veteran of a bad teacher.) My third teacher had me play the most difficult piano material—Richard Addinsell's *Warsaw Concerto*, Frederic Chopin's *Polonaise in A-Flat*, Richard Rodgers' *Slaughter on Tenth Avenue*, Franz Liszt's *Hungarian Rhapsody*—with very little attention to technical skills. While this brought me recognition as a featured artist on radio at age 16, it did not prepare me for the grueling entrance exam to Juilliard. I failed that test. It was only after a year of preparation with a member of the Juilliard faculty that I retook the test and passed. How ironic that I played all that demanding music—but flunked because I couldn't play a scale.

Most teachers recommend that parents wait until their children are already in school before starting piano lessons. Anywhere around the age of 7 and 8 is considered a good starting time. I began at age 5 because I was already playing the piano and church organ. The good sister didn't know that I played exclusively by ear for three years. She played new songs for next week's lesson at the end of each session, not realizing I was storing them in my "ear bank." Each lesson started out by my mimicking every note she played at the last session, and it was only when she asked me to read the music that I got caught.

PLAYING BY EAR

Before going any further, it's important to clear up a few questions about playing by ear. 1. "How do you play by ear?" 2. "Can I be taught to do this?" 3. "What do you mean by 'having a talent'?"

Let's start with the second question first. The truly honest answer, though there is literature to the contrary, is *No!* There is no way to teach people to play by ear. That is a God-given gift that's there to be cultivated. Many people are born with this ability. A perfect example is the surgeon who could play any song he heard but only in the key of E-flat.

I was born with a gifted ear, and my parents became aware of this when I was 3½ years of age. My mother took me to a toy store just prior to Christmas to get some ideas as to what Santa should bring. She watched as I scanned the outside window, bypassing the toys on display, and settled on something I had never seen before. When asked if there was anything I might want, my fixed gaze pointed to *"That."* That was my response. "I want *That.*" It turned out to be a miniature grand piano. My mother was amazed at my answer because she knew I had never seen a piano before. Try as she did, she could not change my mind. Consequently, *"That"* wound up under the tree Christmas morning.

That night, as the family sat around the dinner table, I sneaked into the living room to play my new piano. As I sat on the floor, the fingers of my right hand found the keys to play the first bars of the "Marines' Hymn." In repeating that phrase, my left hand joined the right in search of the correct chord to harmonize the melody. The sounds I heard in my head were transferred to the piano via my ten fingers. In essence, I was "playing by ear." Why I chose this song in the first place is unbeknownst to me. My parents had a recording of it, and I had probably heard it on the radio many times and liked it. How many times I heard it prior to playing it for the first time is anyone's guess.

It goes without saying that the ear acts like a tape recorder that stores arrangements of songs as they're played. How one accurately transfers those melodies and harmonies onto the keyboard without a problem is a mystery. When a wrong note or incorrect chord is played, the ear recognizes this and corrects it. Beyond that, further explanation of how to play by ear defies definition. It's like a psychic phenomenon. How can some people predict future events right down to time and day while others can't? There is only one answer. It's a gift from God.

In actuality, the first two questions were answered simultaneously. My colleagues discovered their gift for music in much the same way and were just as stymied in explaining how it's done. We agreed that one is born with an ear that hears exact pitch and that one cannot *"learn"* a good ear. It's *relative* pitch that can be learned through the study of music theory.

Basic music theory teaches the rudiments of music—notes and their value, clefs, rests, bar lines, time signature, key signature—anything that pertains to music itself. As one advances, a course in ear-training instructs how to find intervals such as a fourth, a fifth, a minor 3rd, or a major 3rd from a given pitch. It also includes sight-reading and singing in a chorus in order to implement and fine-tune this skill.

In a nutshell, those born with perfect pitch can see intervals on a written score and hear and sing them accurately without ear-training. Those who don't have this ability can learn. *Everyone* needs music theory to learn the rudiments of music. This background is especially important for singers and instrumentalists like violinists and trombonists who have to find the notes by ear. Even with my good ear, I had to take a course in ear-training—but for a different reason.

During my first year at Juilliard, Richard Franco Goldman, Jr., of the faculty gave me an ear exam. Mr. Goldman sat at one end of the room facing the piano and I was seated at the far end. He played a chord on the piano and asked me to identify it. My response was, "You played G, B-flat, and D." That was correct, but my answer should have been, "That is a minor chord." The ear heard G, B-flat, and D but couldn't identify a minor chord from a major chord. My problem was a theoretical one. Lessons in theory were never included in my early piano lessons. They should have been. Some theory pertaining to reading music was included, like sharps, flats, rests, etc., but scales and chords were never mentioned. Had I been taught scales and chords and how chords are *derived* from scales, there would have been no problem. A required course called "Literature and Materials of Music" rectified the situation.

Whether you have a good ear or not, you can still learn how to play the piano. Always keep this in mind: a good ear is a *plus*—it is not a *must.* Playing by ear makes things easier when it comes to embellishing a song, but remember, you can *learn* to do this. There are books published that will show you how and that will be addressed in a later chapter.

To answer the third question about "having a talent," let's first define the word. Dictionaries, encyclopedias and Roget's Thesaurus define talent as a gift, genius, a natural or acquired ability, an endowment of superior quality, a special creative or artistic aptitude. Earlier I mentioned pianist Leon Fleischer and the repetitive-stress injury that interrupted his thriving career for so many years. A recent *New York Times* article by Loch Adamson had a segment devoted to Leon Fleischer's career. I was fascinated by a statement his son, Julian, a musician himself, made on *his* concept of talent. Earlier recollections of his father "are of him leaning over the keyboard and practicing." Realizing his father's blinding virtuosity, "I guess I'm sad that I don't have that same crazy, prodigious talent. There is a difference between someone who chooses to perform and someone who comes out of the womb playing the piano. Making music was my father's destiny."

A more analytical comment came from Loch Adamson. "Artists may well be born, but they are also made. As scientists gain insight into the complexities of the brain, it is tempting to ascribe artistic talent, even creativity, to genetic or neurobiological factors. Yet, even if talent and creativity are products of nature, they must still be nurtured, recognized, and supported. Nowhere is this more evident than in families of artists where creativity can seem a form of inheritance and dynamic legacy."

Backing up this idea that artists are products of families, Ruth Richards, a psychologist and psychiatrist at the Saybrook Institute in San Francisco, says, "With the right combination of elements—psychological, social and biological—running in artists' families, there is a real possibility of sparking eminent creativity."

While the above statements are very interesting, I'd like to add something that I truly believe. Just as a good ear is a blessing from God, so is talent in *any* form. Almost everyone has a hidden talent waiting to be released. It makes itself known by that relentless nagging need to *do* something—that craving to *try* something. Frustration occurs when we don't pay attention to this need. I reflected on this craving—this need to express a hidden talent—when I related my first experience at the piano with the "Marines' Hymn." Why did I choose this instrument? How did my untrained fingers find the right keys to play with no prior knowledge? Why did the left hand correlate the correct harmony with the right-hand melody? I still don't have the answer.

Several years ago, I attended a concert in New York City's Avery Fisher Hall given by Russian pianist Yevgeny Kissin. What the reviews by the critics would be was apparent from the moment he started to play. Superlative — extraordinary — incredible — unexcelled — the "young Horowitz" were just a few of the accolades. I found it hard to believe anyone his age—19—could play with such maturity, have as extensive a repertoire and play with a technique that overwhelmed his listeners. Had he been 35—probably—but not at 19. Yet it is so. I heard it myself. On the other hand, Kissin is by no means the exception to the rule. Violinist Midori dazzles the audience with her virtuosity at every performance as does Itzak Perlman, who became an instant success a generation earlier. Today's talent is sometimes on a par with the prodigious composers of an earlier period. The works of great composers like Bach, Mozart, Chopin and Beethoven continue to thrive in concert halls throughout the world and it's artists like Kissin, Midori and Perlman who keep their music alive through their brilliant performances.

Although artists are prolific in every facet of the music industry, they cannot claim exclusive rights to talent. Years ago when I visited the Sistine Chapel in Rome for the first time, I lay face-up on a bench in an attempt to view the masterpiece Michelangelo had created on the ceiling. How he envisioned the breathtaking "The Creation" and painted it to absolute perfection while on his back on a scaffold is mind-boggling. The world of sports is not to be left out either. Baseball legends like Babe Ruth and Mickey Mantle inspired generations of youngsters with their awesome batting power and lightning speed. Lately, golf wiz Tiger Woods took the world by storm by winning the coveted Masters tournament at age 21 with an unheard of 18-under-par score.

Try to imagine what life would be like without the inventions of Albert Einstein, Thomas Edison and Alexander Graham Bell. Undoubtedly, the word "talent" does defy description. There are opinions as to what it is, where it comes from, why some have it and why some don't. My honest opinion is that talent is something that will always baffle us and remain the great mystery we know it to be. But while talent may be ephemeral, *ability* is not. Ability can be taught—and learned.

As children, we are encouraged to take all sorts of lessons after school. There are youngsters who display an exceptional voice or show an aptitude for a musical instrument early on and follow that path. Some choose ballet, others prefer painting or sculpting, and many engage in sports exclusively. Whatever the choice, we start out by looking for someone to teach us. Next to family and friends, teachers are the most important people in our lives. They mold us and prepare us for the future.

My experience with incompetent piano teachers showed how much time can be wasted. The student who came to me with deformed fingers not only wasted time, she also developed needless physical problems. Although the learning process for children and adults is similar, the search for a teacher differs. Adults look for a creative, stimulating activity and *want* to learn, whereas children often take lessons because of parental insistence. The maturity and discipline of adults makes them more patient and better able to take direction than youngsters. In their desire to learn, mature people cover more material in a shorter period of time and reduce the learning process.

In pursuing your search for the right instructor, the following should help you decide who best suits your needs.

- Find someone who prefers teaching adults, not someone who specializes in teaching children.
- Know beforehand what kind of music you are interested in learning. Some teachers teach only classical music, while others teach popular music. The best suited is obviously someone who understands both.
- Interview the teacher, just as an employer interviews prospective workers. Keep in mind that an excellent pianist is

not necessarily an excellent teacher. Look for someone who is confident, forthright, and patient. Remember that if personalities clash, it's not going to work. We change doctors, dentists, and attorneys periodically, so why not teachers?

- Avoid a teacher whose approach is strictly analytical. A competent instructor includes theory, music appreciation, history, technique, and sight-reading into the lesson. There should be some time for review and questions at the end.
- Select someone who is easy to understand and can demonstrate at the keyboard. It's important to explain phrasing and "breathing" between phrases—an integral part of interpretation—and to demonstrate *both* vocally and at the piano. This allows the student to fully grasp the musical meaning of a line.
- A teacher should select technical exercises and repertoire according to the capabilities of the student. For instance, someone with large hands and long fingers is better able to play technically demanding music than someone who is petite. A piano teacher is like a doctor who prescribes medication on an individual basis.
- The teacher should encourage listening to recordings, attending concerts, and playing duets with other performers. By incorporating painting, theater, opera, literature, chamber music, and oratorio (choral work) into life, appreciation of the art world will be elevated to new heights.
- A tutor who has master classes, or allows other students to listen in on a lesson, expands the student's concept through another's interpretation. Playing for our peers instills confidence and prepares us for public performance.
- Personalities and temperaments *must* blend as they must in any relationship. You want someone who will push you, but not too hard—someone who will answer your questions almost before you ask—someone who will instantly recognize your needs.

My teacher at Juilliard, the late Alton Jones, was the ideal teacher for me because he had all the above qualities, plus he understood my hectic schedule and its pressures. My five-hour-a-day commute and three part-time jobs plus the academic/practice schedule often left me too exhausted to take a piano lesson. When it was necessary to cancel, he always arranged a make-up lesson at my convenience. Equally important, he was there when I needed pats on the back and megadoses of encouragement.

Music schools, local colleges, and music stores are excellent sources for finding a teacher because they have a roster available. If you live near a large city, you might find a music teacher registry at the local union office of the American Federation of Musicians. Don't overlook music majors at universities and school alumni who concertize and teach. (See Appendix A.)

You can discern a teacher's ability through his students' performance by attending recitals and concerts. Placing ads stating *your* needs narrows the search because it's personalized. Be sure to specify the time frame that best suits your taking a lesson. Indicate whether or not you can travel for a lesson. A family situation may require the session at home. Post these ads strategically in music stores, schools, colleges, church bulletin boards, supermarkets—any place that attracts a steady stream of people. Have an ad placed at the stage entrance of concert halls where it will be seen by orchestra musicians who teach privately.

ADULT COURSES

Adult courses in music appreciation given in local schools and colleges have been popular with both the newcomer and returnee for many years. At a piano lesson, a student's time is spent learning theory, building a strong technique and expanding the repertoire. By attending music appreciation lectures, one learns about composers and their styles—how individual styles differ, how the musical repertoire unfolded and developed from 12th-century Gregorian chants to the present period, etc. By combining the "hands-on" approach from a piano lesson with knowledge amassed at an adult course, one's education is all-inclusive.

A recent article by pianist Eva Lisa Kovalik in *The Juilliard Journal* relays a story of how Olga Samaroff, a member of the Juilliard piano faculty in the 1930s, started an adult course for the purpose of *enlightening* the concert-going and music-loving public not previously exposed to music education. Years later, one of my teachers, Stanley Wolfe, created the Extension Division for the sole purpose of *educating* the nonprofessional musician. These classes proved so successful that Mr. Wolfe introduced his most popular class, "Music Orientation," to enable people with no background, but a love for music, to learn the fundamentals of listening. These courses are still in progress and have expanded to accommodate the growing demand. It's a wonderful way to grasp the musical outlet missed in earlier years or to brush up on neglected skills.

Adult courses are given all over the world by a faculty of distinguished artists in tune with your needs. They encourage growth and expression in a most supportive and friendly manner. Classes are usually held in the late afternoon and evening and on weekends for the convenience of those who are employed full-time. Such programs include courses in theory, music history, literature, composition, and performance. In the New York/New Jersey/Connecticut tri-state region, accessibility to New York City provides an opportunity to select from ten top-rated schools having adult courses. (See Appendix B.)

If you have a problem locating a teacher because you live in an out-of-the-way area, the prudent thing to do is to contact professional teaching associations for their directory of teachers nationwide. There is also a book available in all libraries with a listing. (See Appendix C.)

Don't give up if your first choice is not to your liking. Don't let the first negative experience put you off. Sometimes it takes a long time to find the right teacher. Once you are content with your choice, put aside a certain amount of practice time each day. Ask questions of your teacher when you don't understand. Stick to this regime and don't get discouraged.

SUPPLEMENTAL LEARNING METHODS

Music stores and libraries now stock their shelves with computer programs for adults as well as teaching videos and sight-reading systems. The right video can be an indispensable tool, especially for someone wanting to recoup what has been forgotten. For a beginner, if used in conjunction with a theory/music book, it's the next best thing to having a teacher present during practice.

I must stress, though, that a teaching video should be used as a *supplement* to a teacher, not as a replacement. Only a teacher can catch the bad habits that unknowingly creep in. A student is so preoccupied learning the craft, he's unaware these habits are being stored to memory subconsciously. Bad hand and wrist positions, slouching posture, inaccurate memorization and inconsistent rhythm are just a few of the things that develop into major problems if not caught in time. Remember the good old school days when the teacher was constantly correcting the class? As teenagers, we have an instructor with us when we learn to drive. The golf pro is there to make sure that stance, hand position and back swing all coordinate for that perfect shot. Every adult education class has a teacher at the helm. From childhood on, we need guidance when we learn something new.

With all the teaching videos available in libraries and music stores, I recommend checking out the rentals and libraries first. Videos can run into considerable money, especially if the package includes more than one tape and is not tailored to your needs. Most videos include theory with hands-on instruction as well as a manual and songbook. The point to remember is *they vary*. Some teach only theory; some combine theory with playing instruction; a few are produced for the modified electronic keyboard while the rest instruct on the full acoustic piano. Read the back of the jacket cover and base your buying decision on where you are at that point and where you want to go.

Once the choice is made, *proceed at your own pace.* You already know the most indispensable gadget in the house is the remote control, and the rewind button its greatest feature. What better teaching tool is there than repetition? Single out the parts that need added attention and then go forward. By singling out stubborn passages at the start, you avoid potential roadblocks ahead. Use this concept with your music book in tow and your teacher as a "checker."

Start at the library by reviewing Kultur's *Let's Play the Piano and All Those Keyboards,* with Bud and Pearl Conway as instructor and demonstrator. This video comes with an instruction manual and songbook and four lessons explaining music theory. By coordinating instruction with demonstration, the presenters explain everything pertaining to music theory in a precise way: names of keys, sharps and flats, triads, scales, reading of the staff, note values, rhythmic notation, how to practice, hand position, etc. This information is then applied to a song. It's excellent for beginners who have no knowledge of theory whatsoever.

For those with a little knowledge of the keyboard, Richard Bradley put together a three-tape series called *How to Play Piano* (VH024). It's highly recommended because of its solid foundation and classical approach. Theory is reviewed before the viewer actually gets to the playing of simple tunes. This might be a little advanced for the true beginner, but certainly one to consider after some basics have been mastered.

The Contemporary Keyboardist—The Basics (VH0112) by

John Novello is another excellent three-tape series and is more jazz-oriented than the aforementioned. Theory is included to help understand the material covered, as is harmony, technical drills, intervals, scales, triads, and ear-training. It is suggested for the beginner to the intermediate student.

The Bradley and Novello tapes are DCI music videos put out by Warner Brothers Publications, Inc., in Miami Beach, Florida (telephone: 1-800-327-7643).

Additional popular teaching videos include:

- *The Ultimate Beginner Series—Keyboard Basics* in two tapes by Larry Steelman.
- *Starter Series—Beginning Keyboard* published by Hal Leonard Corp. in Milwaukee, Wisconsin (telephone: 1-414-744-3630). This is in two volumes with a booklet and live band footage that allows the student to play along.
- *You Can Teach Yourself* is a two-hour video based on the standard piano book by Mel Bay Publications, Inc., of Pacific, Missouri (telephone: 1-800-863-5229). This combination video/audio book is written in an easy-to-understand teaching style that the neophyte takes at his own pace.
- *Anyone Can Play Portable Keyboards* by Mel Bay Publications, Inc., is strictly for keyboards and teaches only the right hand. It has pre-set sustained chords for the left hand and is for people of all ages with no prior knowledge of music. An instructor demonstrates the use of controls and built-in rhythm patterns. Obviously, this is more for fun than anything else.

Once you have conquered the technical and theoretical aspects and are reading music, there's an assortment of tapes lining the shelves from which to choose. If your preference is boogie-woogie, honky-tonk piano, blues, jazz or jazz/rock, or whatever, it's all there waiting for you.

The more music you read, the better your sight-reading becomes. It's like driving a car or playing a sport. Improvement comes with the actual "doing" and repetition. The only instance where a sight-reading tape might be helpful is if there's a learning disorder. Otherwise, it's still "practice makes perfect."

Now congratulate yourself for taking the first steps. You're on your way because you *put* yourself on your way.

SELECTING THE RIGHT LEARNING MATERIAL

From time to time, we find ourselves dashing into a store to purchase an item only to come out without it. We are frustrated because we cannot find exactly what we want due to the overwhelming variety on display. This often happens to the neophyte who attempts to select the right book to teach him/herself to play the piano. The selection is bewildering and the choice better left to an accredited teacher. A professional is your best guide to the studies and etudes appropriate to your level of ability. He/she is well-informed as to the teaching literature available and the new material arriving on the market. Instruction books are abundant and usually come in a series of three or four. For those returning to the piano, books that start with a thorough review are also available.

I spoke to a colleague from Juilliard whose students have played in national competition and we agreed that Alfred's *Basic Adult Piano Course* is our top choice. It is thorough and contains levels one through three in a three-book series. Level three has the ever-popular Beethoven compositions "Moonlight Sonata" and "Für Elise" in their original form. Also available and optional is a CD/cassette that enables the student to hear how each piece in this series should be played. With *The Basic Adult Theory Piano Book,* a student fortifies the theory learned in this series through a written assignment—much like the tests given in our school days.

Later, the student can move on to a series called *Basic Adult All-Time Favorites.* It features classical numbers, folk and country, sing-along favorites, holiday, seasonal, and special-occasion songs in an easy-to-play style. Some selections include lyrics, and all are easy to sight-read.

If a student needs more help with sight-reading and ear-training, Alfred's has material targeted for these specific areas. Other features include a jazz/rock improvisation book and a series of four books for duets. Almost all come with CDs. *Teach Yourself to Play Electronic Keyboard* is for beginners with no prior musical training. It contains easily recognizable songs like "He's Got the Whole World in His Hands," "The Entertainer," "Amazing Grace," and "On Top of Old Smokey." All this material can be purchased at any music store or by contacting Alfred Publishing Company, Inc., 16320 Roscoe Blvd., P.O. Box 10003, Van Nuys, California 91410-0003 (telephone: 1-818-891-5999; fax: 818-891-2369; website: www.alfredpub.com).

Alfred's is only one example of the many comprehensive courses on the market and available throughout the world. On a par with Alfred is a popular two-book series containing the standard learning material plus scales, primary chords and chord dictionary, cadences, music dictionary, and pedal instruction. It's *The Older Beginner Piano Course* and is put out by James and Jane Bastien. Once the student reaches the intermediate level and the basics are well ensconced, text is available on musicianship for the older beginner in *The Bastien Older Beginner Piano Library.* It contains *Easy Piano Classics,* a book selected and edited by James Bastien.

For the returnee, there are two editions I especially like. One, also by Bastien, is called *Piano: Second Time Around.* It can be used privately or at group sessions and is a refresher course that includes technical exercises by Czerny and Hanon, scales, studies, arpeggios, piano literature, reference section, dictionary, list of composers, terms and symbols, and a glossary. Bastien's literature is plentiful in music stores or can be purchased through publisher Neil A. Kjos, Jr., 4382 Jutland Dr., San Diego, California 92117.

My second recommendation is *Elementary Instruction Book for the Pianoforte* by Ferdinand Beyer. It was revised and enlarged by William Scharfenberg, published by G. Schirmer and distributed by Hal Leonard in both English and Spanish. I didn't find this in a music store, but in a large branch of the Barnes and Noble bookstore near Lincoln Center in New York City. It has an excellent brush-up section for the returnee that includes exercises, pieces, and duets to be played with a teacher where parts are interchanged (great for sight-reading) and scales and general technique. While Bastien and Beyer are different in design, they are comprehensive and should be given serious consideration. Seek guidance so that you choose the right course for you. If you start out wrong, you will only have to undo and start again. (See Appendix D.)

The McClintock Piano Course: A New Experience in Learning by Lorene McClintock is a home-study course designed to be used unassisted or with an instructor. The complete package consists of 201 lessons in three volumes of music and eight volumes of text. Included is a keyboard concealer and manuscript book in two boxed sets. A sampling of its contents is Lesson #47, entitled "What Is a Rest? What Is a Slur? What Is a Staccato Note?" This appears to be a well-thought-out program, but its high price for something that may or may not suit your needs should be considered. To get information on The McClintock Piano Course, contact McClintock Enterprises, 853 Seventh Ave., New York, New York 10019 (telephone: 1-800-428-0018; website: www.lorenemcclintock.com).

Books on the market other than textbooks give the reader both general and specific information. While they don't teach you how to play, they can supply answers to the many questions you might have about music. (See Appendix E.)

4

The Importance of Practicing Correctly

You can buy the recommended textbooks and set aside time for practice, rearrange furniture to make room for your new piano, but it will all be in vain without diligent practice. The old saw that "it took twenty years to become an overnight success" refers to the one constant synonymous with success: practice, practice, practice. That, by the way, is also the comedian's reply to "How do I get to Carnegie Hall?" Young gymnasts who compete at the Olympics must put in countless hours of practice every day, as do sports figures and concert artists. Fame and fortune come through hard work, discipline, and patience.

The wonderful thing about learning to play the piano as an adult is that you're not out to compete with the pros. You want to have fun and fulfill that lifelong dream. To do so, though, you, too, must practice. Practice is the *only* road to achievement. Expect discouraging moments; they are part of the learning process. *Stick with it!* Don't give up! Everyone who reached his/her goal has encountered bleak moments along the way. Remember: improvement is assured and guaranteed only if you continue to practice and play on a regular basis.

Several years ago, I gave a seminar at Steinway Hall in New York City for adults already playing the piano and those ready to start. I noticed a man with a despondent face in the audience and approached him during a break. He told me his name was Sam, and he was disheartened about learning. In our conversation, I found out why. He was so anxious to play a song that he totally ignored the first part of Alfred's *Basic Adult Piano Course* and jumped to page 27 to play "When the Saints Go Marching In."

After the session, I asked Sam to follow me to a piano and explained the layout of the basic scale that is graphically explained on page 62 of Alfred's book. It's a formula of five whole-steps and two half-steps that starts on one note and ends on the same tone an octave above. This is a total of eight notes and is the foundation of a scale. This scale can then be played in an ascending/descending pattern including as many octaves as desired. I then explained that a major chord, or triad, is the result of playing the first, third and fifth notes of the scale together. To change the chord from major to minor, lower the third tone one-half step. Chords are also addressed in detail in the same Alfred's book. Within an hour, Sam fully understood the concept of a scale and chords and was able to play them at random as I called out the starting key.

I finished by giving him several technical exercises to practice from Hanon's *The Virtuoso Pianist in 60 Exercises*. By learning the basic scale and how to build a chord, and by practicing these exercises for technique and continuing to learn theory from your chosen course book, you will automatically cut your learning time in half. Soon you will be able to apply this to songs you've always wanted to play.

TIPS FOR THE BEGINNER

- Set aside some time for practice every day. Since schedules fluctuate and interfere with practice sessions, devote as much time as you can *when* you can.

- Overdoing technical exercises can cause untrained muscles and tendons to tighten. Prevent this by practicing for shorter periods at first and gradually increase the time as muscles respond. By overtaxing muscles, you are forcing them to move in ways contrary to the laws of nature. Injuries can result if this goes unheeded.

- Take breaks from time to time. Shake your hands and let your arms hang loose to release any tension that may have built up. Exercises especially good for strengthening, flexibility, and stretching the hand can be found in books by Hanon, Czerny, and Phillip.

- Have your teacher demonstrate the correct hand position on the piano before you start. Improper hand position is not as easy to correct as wrong notes or bad fingering.

- Good posture, correct seating position and height, as well as distance between bench and keyboard should be taken into account.

- Train yourself to be articulate from the start, otherwise you're wasting time and energy. Technical exercises, scales and arpeggios yield the most benefit if practiced with a firm touch and in various tempos.

- Don't exaggerate hand motions as this causes tension and prevents maximum speed.

- Lastly, don't let anyone tell you there is an age limit for technical development. Your hands, wrists, and arms respond just as well to these exercises as your body does to a workout at the gym.

- Combine technical training with the study of theory. In music theory, you learn the symbols and functions of the staff, clefs, notes and their values, key and time signatures, bar lines, measures, rests and dynamics. This is all contained in the first book of your selected series. These symbols are used repeatedly and become ingrained rather quickly. When this is solidly in tow, proceed directly to the keyboard and start making music.

PERSEVERANCE PAYS OFF

Reading music is habit-forming, just like anything else that is repetitive. When I decided to play golf, I took three lessons a week with an excellent golf pro and practiced diligently. The pro was there to catch any mistake from becoming a bad habit. It resulted in my being able to break 100 by the end of the first season. This only happened because I put in a lot of concentrated effort and didn't give up. Apply this to everything you are learning about music and you'll be playing the piano before you know it.

Play at your own pace! When my nieces and nephew were learning how to drive, I accompanied them once in a while as they practiced. They realized early on the need to be comfortable behind the wheel. Whether behind the wheel, at the piano, or on a golf course—set your own pace and stick with it. Increase the tempo only when you gain confidence. Once you have the knack, add sight-reading to your sessions. Start by observing the clefs, time and key signatures, tempo, dynamics, etc. You don't have time for that when you're sight-reading because you're busy reading ahead of what you're playing. Proceed calmly despite mistakes and *don't* stop to correct them. The goal is to do a general reading of the piece and the overall training of the eye and ear.

As your sight-reading takes on a note of confidence and you start working on individual compositions, take passages out of the pieces that are difficult and make an exercise out of it. Play hands separately and in slower tempos until the difficulties are under control. Avoid playing mechanically by including all dynamics and phrasing. Analyze the piece as a whole before you start. An artist does this before even lifting a brush to the canvas. Your first inclination is to mimic the teacher, but eventually your own musical imagination develops and comes to the fore. Once the notes are down, concentrate on phrasing and interpretation. If you visualize what's on the manuscript and hear the phrasing, it'll never leave you.

If you find you are having a problem adhering to tempo on a classical composition, consider purchasing a metronome at your local music store or school-supply store. This mechanical device can be electric, transistor, or wind-up. A metronome is an instrument that resembles a pyramid with a steel pendulum that clicks back and forth at a steady pace. To adjust the tempo or speed, move the adjustable weight on the pendulum up or down. It takes from approximately 40 to 208 beats (or ticks) per minute. ♩ = 120 means weight is adjusted at 120 beats or quarter notes per minute. This is a rigid measurement and shouldn't be taken too literally. The basic principle of a metronome is to stabilize a vacillating tempo. If you develop that inner feeling of rhythm, you will find you won't have to rely on counting or a metronome.

PRACTICE PAYS OFF

You alone will know when you're proficient enough to take that next step. At this juncture, the step-by-step approach has proven to be the only recourse. Theory is now solidly ingrained. Technical exercises have expanded to include *chromatic scales* (a series of half-tones starting on any note and played in either direction) and *arpeggios* (notes of a chord played in rapid succession up and down the keyboard). Segments of practice time put aside for sight-reading have fine-tuned your reading skills and now it's time to tackle memorization.

MEMORIZATION

There is a decided difference between *memorization* and *remembering*. Memorization is mechanical in nature and comes by way of *analyzing* music for structure—*seeing* it on text and *hearing* it. Remembering is basically a state of consciousness and awareness. My Juilliard teacher suggested that on the long train ride to and from school, I place a book on my lap and literally "finger" the composition to be memorized. This forced my mind to hear and see the score as written. In other words, the ear was *hearing* what the eye was *seeing*. The greatest benefit was derived when I played the entire piece in slow motion. Not only was the music being memorized, so was fingering, dynamics and phrasing. If anything prepares one for a performance without music, this does. It's exhausting and requires total concentration, but trust me, it's a true test that guarantees no slip-ups on stage.

Here are several helpful hints to make the memory process easier:

- Instead of memorizing note-for-note, look for patterns, either harmonic or melodic. Anything repetitive is already learned.
- Practice with your eyes closed. It is just as fortifying as practicing away from the piano. You are forced to slow down and concentrate.
- Use the same fingering all the time. As with similar patterns, it's already under your belt.
- Have foreknowledge regarding harmony and intervals. It's indispensable when committed to memory.

Memorizing allows more freedom for interpretation because the physical act of reading is not restricting you. Actors welcome this for that very reason. Phrasing, shading, and rhythm can be observed more intently and freely. The annoying habit of the head "bobbing" between the music on the page and the keyboard is eradicated. Any keyboard, whether the piano, typewriter, or computer, eventually becomes second nature, requiring only limited "sneak-peeks."

Once you've reached this plateau, you should begin to play for others. It's natural to feel nervous, but it does improve play-

ing because of the intense concentration involved. Even sea-
soned pros get the jitters before going on stage. The best way to
hear yourself objectively is to tape yourself. You will hear things
you don't like and correct them. Somehow we seem to be our
own worst critic, so don't carry that too far. Just know you've
come a long way toward fulfilling your dream.

IMPROVISATION

The late jazz violinist, Stephane Grappelli, once described
improvisation as "a mystery like the pyramids. You can write a
book about it but by the end, no one still knows what it is." It's
also been described as "music created while being performed
without any prior preparation." This is a major plus for people
who "play by ear." Jazz musicians often have this natural gift.
They're able to superimpose melodies to harmonic backgrounds
effortlessly. Their fingers relate what their minds hear. Any inhi-
bitions are out the window when it comes to ad-libbing because
freedom is the pivotal concept that permits the flow of creative
juices. The imagination becomes a wide-open spigot permitting
that bottomless well to surge. It doesn't dictate time or length or
dynamics or pattern or repetition.

In an article entitled "Improvisation," Mildred P. Chase re-
lates how saxophonist John Coltrane sometimes practices
silently, just running his fingers over the keys of the instrument
in a meditative state and hearing the music within. A pianist can
do this by practicing improvisation on a digital keyboard without the use of headphones. One is forced to listen as he creates
and experiments. Give it a try. Start with your favorite piece of
music. Improvise around it by changing only the melody and
leaving the harmony alone. Expand upon this and transfer to
the keyboard any musical thoughts you hear in your mind.
Create patterns and combine them with other patterns. There
will be times when the "well will run dry," but don't give up. Try

later. Be free to explore like a curious child. Change tempo, include pauses, change moods, pick out sequences, recognize repetition. *Experiment as you go!* Some results you will like, others will drop by the wayside.

This is also an excellent way to train the ear. Play a note and look away from the keyboard as you play intervals. Define them and continue this study. Make a melody out of it. Tape it and don't be surprised if you have the makings of a musical hook for a song.

Mildred Chase suggested experimenting on the black keys alone. The pattern of three black keys, then two black keys is the root of the F-sharp 6 chord. This is described in your theory book. Leave the pedal down and go to work. You can't make a mistake. As a child, remember how you and your friends learned "I Love Coffee, I Love Tea" and "Chopsticks" by rote? You alternated and played both the base and treble parts as a duet.

Jazz musicians have made it a point over the years to listen to their idols, both live and on tape, and to imitate them. They learned from their peers that this is the best route to finding an individual style. By picking and choosing from others, plus incorporating your own ideas, you carve a niche for yourself that is your signature.

FAKE BOOKS

As you advance and master reading music and chord structure, you will be ready for *Fake Books.* They are quite different from a regular collection book. A collection book has music written out on *both* staves, while a fake book has *only* the melody line of a song written out on *one* staff. Chord symbols are written above the notes. Both types of books include the composers, the shows the songs are from, and lyrics, if any. Fake books are officially called "Fake Books" and can be found in music and book stores around the country. At one time they were illegal because royalties were not paid on the published works. That law changed when they became such an important part of a performer's library. They are now heavily stocked in most stores. Included are standard, show, and Latin-American tunes; songs of the Gay Nineties, foreign, gospel, holiday, and folk songs; marches, pop, rock, jazz, country—all you will ever need. There is even a book on classical music and operatic arias called *Song Dex Treasury of World Famous Instrumental Music,* compiled and edited by George Goodwin. Today, individual song sheets cost several dollars. The going rate for a fake book is between $20 and $50 and it is written for piano, organ, portable keyboards, guitar, and vocals. Believe me, that is a bargain.

Whether you are interested in classical or popular music or both, music shelves literally bulge at the seam with every resource imaginable. Sheet music and books (including fake books) abound from country to classical to operatic to Broadway musicals to rock-and-roll to jazz. If you want to zero in on a specific area, you'll have no problem locating the music for two piano–four hands, duets for one piano, big-band hits, books for electronic keyboards, chamber music, or oratorio. The list is endless, as you can see. (See Appendix F.) Don't be intimidated by all of this. Your teacher will guide you, as will your peers and your instincts.

Now that you are totally saturated and overwhelmed by what's available, the question is where to find it. It is virtually impossible to keep abreast of music stores nationwide, as they open and close at random. Check your local music and book stores and branches of national book stores like Barnes & Noble and Borders. They always have a selection in stock and upgrade and restock regularly. There are three music stores in New York City and one major publishing company with two branches in Pennsylvania. (See Appendix G.)

LISTEN TO THE GREAT PIANISTS

Those of you who grew up in the days of Tin Pan Alley probably still have vinyl records around the house of favorite singers and musicians. The forties and fifties produced many great songs, singers and bands, so dust those records off and pull out the turntable. They are an important adjunct to your musical education. So much is absorbed by listening to these artists for style, phrasing and tempo. I have many favorite pianists, including Art Tatum, Oscar Peterson, Marian McPartland, Barbara Carroll, Nat King Cole, George Shearing and Tommy Flanagan. One day, I told Marian how I wore out her recording of Harold Arlen's "It's Only a Paper Moon," as well as my mother's living room carpet, by running back and forth between the stereo and piano, transcribing it note for note. Her style impressed me because it was clean and creative in its use of harmonic chords and phrasing. Her improvisation was easy to follow. The same holds true for Barbara Carroll, who, with Bobby Short, has been ensconced in New York's Carlyle Hotel for many years. Barbara is the epitome of elegance, and her playing is extremely creative and tasteful.

George Shearing's style differs in that he relies heavily on block chords in his first chorus. Improvisation follows before he finishes the tune in his unique style. Listen to his arrangement of "Lullaby of Birdland" and it's evident. Oscar Peterson and Art Tatum will floor you with their technical dexterity. Their hands are one big *whir* on the keyboard. Fats Waller once spotted Tatum in the audience and, looking straight at him, told the audience, "I play piano, but 'God' is in the house tonight." Nat King Cole is pure genius because of his simplicity and elegance. Listen to his solo work and vocal accompaniment. When singing, his playing is understated. When he returns to soloing, he does so with fervor. Another "gentleman of the keyboard" is Tommy Flanagan. I've been following Tommy ever since his days as Ella Fitzgerald's pianist and arranger. As an accompanist, he is superb. As a featured artist, the ultimate.

These giants of piano were my role models. They taught me style and interpretation. Select performers you especially like. Be able to say, "Aha! That's what I want to sound like. That's what I *can* sound like." The more artists you listen to, the quicker you will develop a style. It's like paraphrasing. The dictionary defines paraphrase as "to express the meaning of a passage in different words." Put together the musical nuances you favor, mix and match as we do in fashion, and you will soon emerge with a style of your own.

Do the same with classical music. Insert tapes of the legendary masters like Horowitz and Rubinstein into your Walkman when lying on the beach or flying 35,000 feet in the air. The tape deck of your car is an ideal place to listen to performances of today's artists like Yefim Bronfman, Peter Serkin and Richard Goode. Long trips become less tedious and you're learning along the way. As with popular music, your sense of interpretation, phrasing and color will take on an added luster. Never stop learning, listening or practicing. It's life's greatest tonic.

5

Know About Pianos Before Selecting One

The original piano was invented by an Italian harpsichord maker, Bartolomeo Cristofori, in 1709. He bridged the gap between harpsichord and piano by designing a new hammer action that made the keys more pliable for control and dynamics. The British called it a pianoforte and the Europeans, a fortepiano. The name introduced the dynamic range symbols—**p** (piano) for soft and **f** (forte) for loud—to piano literature. Early in the next century, around the time of Liszt and Chopin, the instrument became the piano as we know it today. Ironically, the keyboard has been called the world's first bar code because of its easily understood pattern of two and three black keys.

Several years ago, I gave a seminar at Steinway Hall in New York City for adult beginners and re-starters. This was sponsored by the world-famous piano company, Steinway and Sons. In preparing for this series, Steinway supplied me with a lot of information about the piano—much of which I didn't know. As this chapter unfolds and I pass this information on, you can use it as a guide to help you to select the right piano for you. But first, here is a brief history of the Steinway piano family.

Steinway and Sons was established in New York in 1853 by Heinrich Engelhart Steinway and his sons. Their first instrument, the square grand piano, was replaced by the modern grand in 1856 and followed by the upright. The company started marketing in London in 1870, and in 1880, a branch factory was opened in Hamburg, Germany. Steinway became the first American product to be favorably recognized in Europe. During this time span, a factory was built in Astoria, Queens, and remains there today. The original Steinway Hall was a large concert hall seating 2,500 and was erected in 1866 on 14th Street in New York City. The present showroom on 57th Street opened in 1925.

Theodore Steinway, the eldest of Heinrich's sons, was the company's engineer and was largely responsible for the Steinway of today. All Steinway pianos are handcrafted in Astoria and Hamburg, taking about one year for completion. The New York company produces about 2,500 pianos annually while the Hamburg branch produces 2,000. Steinway retains its reputation as the piano most widely requested in the world because it has virtually remained unchanged since its inception. Many hands go into building and installing the more than 12,000 parts that make up each grand piano. This accounts for its incomparable craftsmanship, unique sound, distinctive characteristics, and exquisite detail. Today, up to 95 percent of concert artists worldwide make Steinway their piano of choice.

The fact that a grand piano has over 12,000 parts is in itself mind-boggling. That it is entirely handcrafted, using no power tools whatsoever, is truly amazing. Several years ago, an article in the *New York Times* Metro section by Michael T. Kaufman, entitled "The Team That Builds Steinways," explained how the rim of the grand piano is made: "Six strong men glue together 22-foot-long strips of matched maple to form a piece of laminated wood weighing about 600 pounds. They carry it on their shoulders to a special bench where they pull and wedge and clamp, bending the 18-ply thickness into the curvaceous shape of a grand piano. They are producing the sturdy frame of a concert grand piano costing $60,000." This system of bending strips of maple to create the rim of the piano has become rare. The cost of materials, plus the necessary aging and drying process to bend together both inner and outer rims to form one rim, has become prohibitive. Is it any wonder the price of pianos escalates on a regular basis? The latest price range has the nine-footer nearing $80,000.

Steinway also improved and patented the "overstrung grand." They ran the bass strings over the treble strings and spread them into a fan shape. This permitted placement of the bridge into the center of the soundboard allowing it to vibrate more freely. The result was greater volume, a stronger singing treble, and a powerful bass. Steinway meticulously developed a better way to fasten the strings and the best way of transmitting the player's touch to a hammer being thrown against the string.

As we discuss the structure of a piano and learn about its components, regard for the instrument only escalates. The same holds true for many things we take for granted. Awareness escalates when we observe the workmanship in items used every day, like a toaster, a coffeemaker, and a stove. We wouldn't have them if someone hadn't conceived the idea, perfected it and marketed it. What about balls used in popular sports like base-ball, tennis, golf and soccer? Someone conceived the idea, but how many minds went into the process of custom-designing them for the individual sport? They differ in size, weight, composition and jacket, yet they're all round. Like the piano, they have to meet the same high standards before leaving the factory for marketing.

The piano components to be discussed are in alphabetical order, making it convenient for future reference. Concurring numbers in the diagram identify the location of the components described. The function of each component is explained in "layman's language." This information will be invaluable when you shop for your piano.

- *Action:* (1) The action of a piano consists of all the intricate parts that convey the motion of the key to the hammers that strike the strings and the dampers that mute them. The action, which is under the soundboard and mounted on a keyframe, varies with the size of the piano. Longer strings result in greater volume, resonance and harmonic content. If the action is uneven, it could be because the keys are not weighted properly. The keys and hammers must respond quickly, evenly and easily when touched. In action regulations, adjustments are made to screws, wires, hammers, pedals and dampers. Inspect thoroughly before purchase.

- *Bridge:* (4) There are two bridges—the treble and the bass. The bass bridge is much shorter than the treble bridge and is positioned near the center of the soundboard. They are concave in design. They are made of maple, lie beneath the strings, and are glued to the soundboard. The function of bridges is to transfer the vibrations from the strings to the soundboard. If not transmitted clearly, the tone quality will be inferior.

- *Dampers:* (between 2 and 3) They are the felt pads and wedges that rest against the strings to stop vibration. With the exception of the very top register, a tone is sustained until the damper is released. Strings vibrate when struck by a hammer and the sound is amplified by the soundboard producing a note. To check for damper alignment, press down sustaining pedal and observe the line. They should all lift at the same time.

- *Hammers:* (2) Hammers are wool felt-covered wooden mallets made of maple and birch that strike three wire strings in the treble and two copper strings in the bass. Very low notes have one copper string. If hammers have deep grooves or are warped, they are worn and should be sandpapered down, resurfaced, or replaced.

- *Hitch Pins:* (8) Strings are looped onto steel hitch pins embedded into the cast-iron plate along the curved edge of the piano. These strings are then stretched to the tuning pins fastened into the pinblock in front of the instrument.

- *Keytops:* They cover the Bavarian spruce keys and come in ivory and plastic. They rest in a spruce keyframe located between the keyboard and keybed. The keyframe guides the keys. In grand pianos, it slides in conjunction with the use of the soft pedal and remains put in vertical pianos. There are 88 keys—52 white and 36 black. Ivory has an irregular natural-grain look, but has been restricted since 1955 because slaughter of elephants for their tusks has been outlawed. In 1989, ivory keys were completely discontinued. Plastic keytops are clear with no grain and can be replaced at moderate cost. Black keys can be made of ebony wood or hard plastic. To clean the keys, use lightly dampened cheesecloth only and never solvents. Don't allow any water to seep between the keys to the keybed as it will cause swelling and hamper the mobility of the keys. If ivory keys absorb moisture, they could curl and fall off.

- *Pedals:* (9)

    (A) The *sustaining* or *damper pedal* on the right lifts dampers off strings, causing notes played while the pedal is down to continue ringing out. When the pedal is released, make sure the dampers fall back against the strings, completely stopping the sound. If the pedal squeaks, the fault could be in the wooden rods leading to the damper rod. All pedals are made of heavy, solid brass.

    (B) The *soft pedal* on the left softens the sound by shifting the action and keyboard to the right, striking two strings out of three. In an upright, hammers move closer to strings, requiring less force. "Una-corda" dates back to a time when there were only two strings in the piano as opposed to today's three.

(C) The *sostenuto pedal* or middle pedal sustains the notes in the bass played prior to depressing the pedal. It does not affect the upper register except in Steinway pianos. It's used mostly by accomplished pianists playing classical music. The center pedal in old vertical pianos was employed as a means of lowering and raising a silencer (a felt strip that lowered and was positioned between hammers and strings to mute the sound). It enabled one to practice quietly. Now it's an added feature.

- *Pinblock* (7), a/k/a wrestplank, is a hardwood laminated plank made of maple running the width of the piano and integral to the rim. Steel tuning pins are anchored in holes in the pinblock. Strings are coiled around these pins and looped onto hitch pins at the lower end of the plate. To tune the piano, a tuning hammer increases or decreases tension on the string to harmonize with one another.

- *Pitch* is the number of vibrations per second necessary to produce a given sound. In tuning, the correct pitch is established by matching a tuning pipe or fork regulated to A 440. In other words, if in tune, a tone cycles 440 times per second when a hammer strikes a string. All orchestral instruments are tuned to this concert pitch. Some instruments, like strings and brass, are flexible and can vary in pitch. Some instruments, like the clarinet and cornet, can't. Therefore, for uniformity all instruments must conform to concert pitch.

- *Plate:* (6) The plate is made of cast iron with a bronze finish and rests over the soundboard and pinblock. Wood dowels placed around the perimeter prevent the plate from touching the soundboard. Hitch pins are attached to the far end of the plate that supports nearly 35,000 pounds per square inch of string tension pulled over it from the pinblock.

- *Rims:* (10) There are two rims—an inner and an outer. The soundboard is glued to the inner rim and the cast-iron plate supported by dowels rests on it. The rim is made of layers of straight-grained wood anywhere from 13 to 25 feet in length and glued together. Metal presses are used to bend them into one continuous rim. The outer rim is glued to the inner and encases the piano.

- *Soundboard:* (5) It's the heart and soul, or amplifier, of the piano and of utmost importance. It is shaped like a diaphragm in the center to give freedom of movement and lasting tonal response. The center is thicker in construction and tapers as it approaches the rim. An out-of-tune problem arises from the fact the strings don't rise and fall in pitch uniformly. A laminated soundboard (wood layered to prevent splitting and warping) prevents some problems, but the solid Alaskan Sitka Spruce used by Steinway has much more resonance due to its unusual stability and vibration. The soundboard, supported by strips of lightweight wood called ribs, is fitted and anchored into its case along with the cast-iron plate. It has hard rock-maple bridges doweled and glued to it to hold individual string bearings. The vibration of the strings is then transmitted to the soundboard.

- *Strings:* (3) A piano has about 230 strings stretched at high tension across a cast-iron frame. Multiply the average string tension by 230, and the overall tension is about 20 tons. The lower bass notes have one string with one end attached to a hitch pin and the other coiled around a tuning pin. There are two strings for every bass note and a total of three for each treble note. The thickest and longest strings are in the bass and shorten and compress as they advance up the keyboard. The pitch is altered by tightening or relaxing tension. Strings in the treble section are made of steel and the bass strings of steel-core wire wound with pure copper.

- *Voicing:* It affects the piano's tone and quality of sound. By adjusting the density of the felt, you can increase or decrease the brightness. Hammer felts are softened when too harsh and hardened when too mellow. This can be remedied by "needling" the hammer with a felt pick. This should return the original elasticity to the hammer. Final voicing is done in your home and voiced according to the room's acoustics.

KNOW YOUR INSTRUMENT

Take this information about the components of a grand piano and open the lid and fallboard (lid covering keyboard.) Now, one by one, locate the parts discussed. Press one key at a time and observe the hammer action. Press the sustaining pedal and watch the dampers lift off the strings. Play several keys with the damper suppressed and notice how the tone carries on even without fingers on the keys. Release the pedal and the tone stops. Take notice of the action shifting when the soft pedal is suppressed. Play a key with and without the soft pedal down and hear the difference in dynamics. Also, carefully examine how the strings are coiled around the tuning pins anchored in the holes of the pinblock. Pull gently on the string and feel the tension. It's easy to understand how it drops in pitch and goes out of tune as the tension is eased. Study the overall structure of the hammers, soundboard, bridges, dampers, and hitch pins.

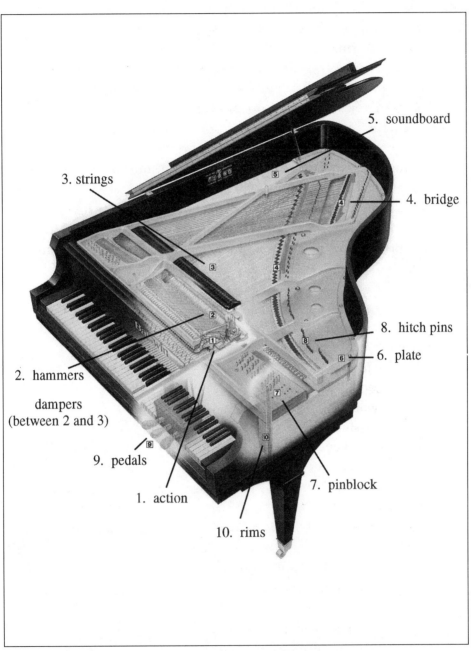

The Anatomy of a Grand Piano

(*Courtesy of:* Baldwin Piano and Organ Company, Mason, Ohio.)

Armed with this knowledge, you will be able to walk into any showroom and exude confidence and poise. You know what to look for, and your sales representative will immediately recognize this acumen. You now understand that what is under the lid of a piano is just as important as what's under the hood of a car. It is not just another pretty item. Pianos are big-ticket items costing many thousands of dollars and are expected to provide excellent service for many years. Needless to say, all parts must be in tip-top shape and work in unison to achieve that goal.

There are parts of a piano unrelated to the primary function that need the same careful scrutiny before making that final decision. Below are checkpoints—questions to ask the dealer and examine yourself.

- Are the strings solid copper or copper-plated?
- Is the fallboard loose?
- Does the music stand wobble?
- Are the legs sturdy?
- Do the pedals function smoothly?
- Is the pedal lyre firm or loose?
- Are the strings rusty?
- Does every key respond properly or do some stick?
- Is the action too stiff?
- Is the veneer loose due to dryness, dampness, or water damage?
- Is the soundboard cracked? If so, reject that piano immediately.
- Are the piano lid's hinges secure?
- When trying out a piano, notice the difference in tone when the lid is up and when it's closed.
  (a) Does it have a rich, velvety sound?
  (b) Are there overtones?
  (c) Is the sound metallic?

Remember, you are buying an expensive item and it's usually a once-in-a-lifetime purchase. Even though you have accrued a lot of information about the instrument, I strongly urge you to retain the service of a skilled piano technician before making a final decision—someone who knows the "ins and outs" and can pinpoint hidden flaws.

PROPER PLACEMENT OF PIANO

There are many things to take into consideration, such as piano placement, conditions, color, and finance, before contacting the technician. You probably have the perfect place in mind for your piano, but let me warn you beforehand. A piano, though a sturdy piece of furniture, is extremely susceptible to climatic changes, especially humidity. It must be kept away from the air conditioner, heater, ceiling vents, damp basements, and uninsulated outside walls. Being in the line of a draft and too close to a working fireplace is also a no-no. Placing it in front of a large picture window may be the ideal spot, but do you want direct sunlight to bleach the wood and ruin the finish? If you must position your piano this way, close the curtains during the time of direct rays or use special blinds to filter out the sun.

If you live near the sea, salt air automatically guarantees rust and corrosion as well as an inordinate number of tunings. I witnessed this at the now defunct Guy Lombardo's East Point House in Freeport, Long Island. Guy purchased a Steinway concert grand for the upper deck, to be used by the pianists in the dance bands employed throughout the years. Even though the windows were closed most of the time, the piano eventually deteriorated and had to be replaced. Your piano dealer may have ways to circumvent this situation, but salt air is a real killer. As you can see, alone or combined, these elements can cause premature structural damage—warped wood, cracked soundboard, unglued parts, lackluster varnish and rusty strings and pins. You can also incur excessive string tension as well as warped and sticking keys. Constant fluctuation between temperature variations and humidity is bad for the overall health of your piano. Keeping the indoor thermostat set at 68 degrees on a yearly basis is a positive step.

SELECTING THE RIGHT PIANO

The next consideration is the size of the room and the type of piano that's appropriate. Vertical pianos, from the largest to the smallest, are *uprights*, *studios*, *consoles* and *spinets*. I would definitely suggest a "taller" piano because the longer the strings, the richer the tone. Verticals stand between 45 inches and 52 inches and are approximately 5 feet wide and 2½ feet deep. Allow another 2 feet for the bench plus 2½ feet to sit, and the overall space required is about 5 feet by 4½ feet. On the other hand, a baby grand, being horizontal, extends anywhere from 4½ feet to 5½ feet, while a medium grand ranges from 5½ feet to 7½ feet. The nine-footer is a concert grand with a majestic sound and is used mainly in concert halls. If your living room is large, a seven-foot grand is both elegant and impressive and will provide a lush sound.

If you want a grand piano, but only have room for a console or spinet, that narrows the search. If you do have the room, a grand is not only a graceful instrument, but has the advantage of a lid that folds back and can be raised two different positions via pegs for volume control. Acoustics plays a significant role in tonal quality, as does the touch of each individual playing the same piano. Different hands, fingers and musculature determine that. An upright's sound tends to bounce out or remain boxed in because of its close proximity to the wall. If the sound needs to be altered, the piano can be placed on a thick rug for sound absorption. A rug could also be hung on the wall behind the instrument. A beautiful color-coordinated tapestry or heavy fabric may be an alternative choice.

COLOR AND CARE

Choosing a color is the easiest part of the entire process because there is such a wide selection. Obviously, you will want something to blend with the room's decor. All pianos come in a satin or high-polish finish. The color choice is mahogany, ebony, oak, cherry, white, ivory, or walnut. Shimmel Piano Company advertises one in plexiglas. New colors arrive on the market regularly, so do your research thoroughly before selecting. Better pianos have higher quality wood in their rim and use only top-grade varnish and lacquer as finishing materials. Use a damp cheesecloth to remove dust and prints from the exterior and wipe with the grain in a straight line only—never a circular motion. Waxing is not recommended. Periodically, the interior of your piano needs attention due to exposure to dust and dirt beyond your control. Small items like pencils, coins and hairpins can fall deep inside the piano and need to be removed professionally.

Be careful when placing objects like vases and pictures on top of the piano. Use a mat or scarf underneath. Dents, scratches and stains from drinks are difficult and costly to remove and may well turn out to be permanent.

PIANO TECHNICIAN

You will come to realize that your piano technician is as vital to your instrument as your mechanic is to your car and your physician to your health.

- A tuner adjusts the action for pitch and voices for restoration of tone. He then regulates the entire action for balance.
- A technician is a *mechanic as well as a tuner*. He repairs, rebuilds, reconditions, restrings and must be thoroughly acquainted with all types of pianos, their parts and assembly. Often, professional pianists and teachers know little about the technical aspects of a piano. What they *do* know is the value of their technician.

To find a reliable technician, contact major piano companies like Steinway, Baldwin, and Yamaha, and prominent music schools like Juilliard in New York, the Curtis Institute in Philadelphia, and the Peabody in Baltimore. Major universities and colleges with music departments have a roster at their disposal, as do music and teaching organizations. Local piano dealers, the yellow pages, and ads in magazines and newspapers will offer a list, but the best recommendation comes from the aforementioned and word-of-mouth. If the first person isn't satisfactory, keep searching. Eventually a technical ally will come along with whom you are comfortable and who will forewarn you of any potential problem on a piano you may already own or are about to buy. Remember: you're new at the game—he's not.

FINANCING

If a new piano is beyond your financial reach at this time, ask your technician about a reconditioned or rebuilt instrument. It can be on a par with a new instrument and does carry a similar guarantee. Just keep this in mind: What's considered "rebuilt" by one may be considered "reconditioned" by another. Pianos no longer used in private homes, as well as other pre-owned pianos, can be found on the Internet and classified ads. Situations do occur where major moves across country or out of the country prove so exorbitant that it's more expedient to buy a new piano once relocated. Also, check piano dealers for instruments that are traded in for different models and makes. You may find just what you're looking for. In all cases, the opinion of a good technician is vital prior to a purchase decision. He might find the soundboard cracked, the felt padding of the hammers worn out, the three pedals and brass support rods not working. He'll check the condition of the keybed, pinblocks, tuning pins, strings, and action and advise you accordingly. Whatever his fee, it is well worth it. You want to feel comfortable with your purchase. Avail yourself of an expert second opinion if you feel the slightest hesitation. After all, this is a major investment.

THINGS TO AVOID

There are three things that are a no-no under any circumstance and they are self-explanatory.

- Avoid buying a used piano from a school or institution. It is usually pretty well beaten up and beyond repair.
- Never buy an instrument unseen, such as one in a factory or warehouse.
- Avoid a 64 key instrument or any piano without the full 88 keys. As your skills expand, you'll need those missing keys.

TUNING

The recommended tuning is twice yearly—when the heat goes on and when it goes off. More tunings are needed shortly after the delivery of a new piano because new strings tend to stretch as the instrument is adjusting to new conditions. Tunings also depend upon use and abuse. A concert artist who practices several hours a day and has an ear pitch of A 440 requires more tunings. Occasionally, a tuner makes minor adjustments to the instrument during the intermission of a performance.

Benches vary in size, style and width, but only an adjustable artist bench or chair can regulate height. The artist bench is the type most often used at concerts. It has knobs on both sides making adjustment easy. The standard bench can accommodate two people and often includes space to store music. Cushions are available for benches that are not padded.

"WHEN IN DOUBT, DON'T"

My guideline, when uncertain about buying for whatever reason, is *rent before buying*. Many people feel apprehensive when they start or return to the piano and doubt their degree of commitment. They also realize that not every piano serves everyone equally well, and the original acquisition may not be the instrument they'll want later on. Another point—you should learn how to play and get the basics under your belt before focusing on sound, touch and tonal quality. Tone, as you learned, is produced through pushing down a key that automatically throws a hammer against a string. Every player gets a different sound from the same piano because each individual has a different touch. As you play, listen for a clear, rich, velvety sound that resonates. Notice whether the action is too heavy or too metallic. Check for a treble that is pure and articulate and a bass that rings out. It's a good idea to bring a professional pianist or teacher along to guide you as you try out various models and makes. Take turns alternating at the keyboard. This will give you the opportunity to observe the traits mentioned and to hear the piano's resonance. Play only a tuned piano before making your decision.

As for acquiring a piano, you have a number of purchase and rental options open to you. Obviously, your financial situation will dictate to a large degree which option you pursue. The good news is that purchasing or renting a piano does not have to be expensive. You can buy a used or restored instrument, rent with the option to buy, finance with a 10 percent minimum down payment, or buy outright.

Before deciding the best route to take, calculate the purchase price, installment interest, tunings, and periodic piano regulations into the overall cost. At this point, remember an investment in a better piano recoups much of the original cost at sale time. Also, when making an investment in grand models like a Steinway B or D, the leaning is to buy new. To save money, sway toward a used or rebuilt model in smaller pianos. Pianos made in the United States and Germany—like Steinway, Baldwin, Beckstein and Bosendorfer—are more expensive than those made in Asia because they are handcrafted. The Yamaha and Kawai of Japan and Young Chang of Korea are leaders in the mid-priced piano market because they are mass-produced.

Renting a piano can be very reasonable with the rent you pay applied to eventual purchase price. A 5- to 15-year warranty is part of the package. Some warranties are transferrable to subsequent owners covering parts, labor and defects in materials. It does not include your periodic tunings and action and tone regulation. Ask your retailer to show you the warranty and the manufacturer's booklet of service recommendations before purchase. The serial number found near the tuning pins denotes the year the piano was manufactured. Jot it down and check your warranty to be sure the right piano is being delivered. Your dealer also carries a booklet called the *Pierce Piano Atlas,* which lists names, serial numbers and year of manufacture of instruments both American and foreign. It's a good source of reference.

THE STEINWAY OPTION PLAN

For those of you who have dreamed of owning a Steinway, that dream may not be as far-fetched as you thought. Steinway has an interesting option called "Six Month Get-Acquainted Rental Program." You have the opportunity of renting a Boston piano designed by Steinway and Sons for six months. The "Boston" is considered Steinway's mid-range instrument. It's less expensive and uses the same materials as a regular Steinway. Once you decide your aptitude for the piano or realize how much you've missed it, all rental costs can be applied toward any new Boston or Steinway piano.

MOVING YOUR PIANO

If you have to move your piano, it's best to leave this to a professional mover. Major companies like Steinway, Baldwin, and Yamaha have shipping departments within their firms and are in a position to export anywhere in the world. Local dealers have their own system and include the shipping fee in the overall cost. Pianos, being delicately balanced instruments, require special packaging and strong, skilled arms in the process. The costs incurred include insurance, damage claims, storage and, if applicable, import duties.

For a private mover, contact your local piano dealer for recommendations. If you're using a large, well-known moving company, they may have the special equipment needed to move the instrument with other large pieces of furniture. Any move, especially cross-country, is expensive, so research thoroughly. Whatever your choice, go with the experienced mover. It may cost a little more, but your instrument will still be intact when it reaches its destination. Be insured at all costs and *don't* move the piano yourself.

DIGITAL/ELECTRONIC KEYBOARDS

No one can deny that we're solidly into an age of synthesized, computerized, amplified and micro-chipped instruments. I recently walked out of two New York stores that specialize in electronic keyboards absolutely spellbound. Salespeople "piled on" brochures, and I read and absorbed this information. But while electronic pianos have come a long way and gained a stronghold in the music industry, their quality can never completely match that of a fine acoustic (traditional) piano. They may, however, constitute an option you'll want to explore.

Amplifying piano strings by placing a magnetic pickup under them started more than sixty years ago in Germany. After World War II, electronic technology, a/k/a the "computer," began its meteoric rise worldwide. In 1991, Yamaha brought the piano into the computer age with its Disklavier—an attachment equipped with optic sensors and a computer. The Disklavier plays and sounds very much like a regular piano, connects to a synthesizer, records what you play, and then plays it back. A synthesizer creates the basic elements of sound electronically and allows you to mix them together. It can alter the sound from that of a piano to that of almost any instrument or sound desired. In playing back, the keys of the instrument move up and down like the old-fashioned player piano. Technology has now reached the point where we only have to press a button, move a lever, or dial a knob to have instant access to whatever information or sound we want.

MUSIC SYSTEMS

There are systems made exclusively for the acoustic piano that allow the instrument to be *silenced* and *heard solely* by the player. The size and design of these systems are similar to the standard-size VCR. They come with headphones and can be fastened underneath the keyboard or placed on top of the piano. What an asset for apartment dwellers in congested cities like New York, Chicago and Boston. The neighbors aren't annoyed, and you are at ease to practice well beyond the imposed curfew. Your spouse can have the television or computer going and you'll never disturb one another. Children can play in the same room or do homework while you silently practice and keep an eye on them. This could also entice the youngsters into taking lessons themselves, knowing they don't have to be self-conscious about practicing. If you purchase a unit with dual headphone jacks or a "Y" cable that has one jack and two cables (a/k/a "splitter"), a teacher can give lessons in your home without interrupting anyone during the session.

Music Systems Research manufactures two systems that make this freedom possible. They are the GT-90 Quiet Time Piano and the Piano Digital GT-360. Both systems add the features of an electronic or digital keyboard to an acoustic piano. It's your choice to play *silently* via stereo headphones or *audibly* via amplified speakers. Included are features that can add orchestral accompaniment to your playing. The piano is silenced by activating a small lever on the unit that dampens the strings with a padded mute rail, stopping the hammers from making direct contact. This does not interfere with the motion or feel of the action.

Both units give the acoustic piano many digital features. The GT-90 activates the following by simply touching a button.

- 16 different instrument selections
- 32-note polyphony

- reverb and chorus
- 3 preset sound combinations
- ability to layer instruments for 40 sound combinations
- 2 headphone jacks
- demo feature

The more sophisticated GT-360 adds these features to the above list.

- 128 instrument selections
- keyboard and velocity splits, tuning, and pitch transposition
- 29 sound presets
- 16 MIDI (Musical Instrument Digital Interface) channels
- built-in metronome

For contact information, see Appendix H.

DIGITAL PIANOS: THE POSITIVE FEATURES

There is a difference between music systems and digital keyboards. Both contain many of the same features, but the systems are *bought separately* and used *in conjunction* with an acoustic piano. A digital keyboard is *one unit only,* containing both keyboard and features.

When professional musicians, especially concert pianists, purchase a *digital* piano, they use it as a *supplement* to the acoustic piano rather than a *replacement* for it. On concert tours, musicians don't always have access to a piano for practice, so the electronic keyboard serves the purpose. Being portable and small, it can be carried and placed on a flat surface or on an adjustable stand and played silently with headphones plugged into the jack. These musicians prefer the standard 88 keys, but smaller keyboards abound, some with 37, 61, and 76 keys. When learning how to play and contemplating the purchase of a digital, go for the 88 keys. You will need it if you stay the course, and the difference in price is well worth it. In the event you sell or replace the keyboard, the sale will be facilitated because of the full set of keys. Digital pianos come with pedals, but the stand and adjustable bench are optional.

Because they're portable, these instruments can be taken on the road, used outdoors, and even taken aboard yachts. Just think—you can practice Chopin on the high seas. Have you ever thought about giving a keyboard as a gift to a loved one in a nursing or adult home? What a wonderful way to idle away lonely hours in cramped quarters! Electronic instruments never go out of tune, regardless of the temperature or humidity, and are virtually maintenance-free. They come with a built-in metronome and a panel of instrumental voices such as harpsichord, vibes, strings, brass, pipe organ and bass, from which to select your own combination. Digital reverbs and pitch controls, built-in rhythm styles, a drum kit, track-recording sequencer, plus a "minus-one" feature are also included. Some even have a "transpose" control so you can play in any key without changing your fingering. Your playing can be stored on a floppy disk for playback and there's also a karaoke feature for sing-along fun. All of this just by touching a button, slipping in a cartridge, or selecting a menu. Amazing!

Depending upon the model and style, prices start around $400 and escalate into the upper four figures. The leading makers of digital pianos are Yamaha, Roland, Korg and Alesis. They make full-sized spinets and grand-shaped pianos with pedals and a choice of finishes, including wood grain. Technology has made dramatic headway in regard to the actual touch of the keys. At one time, the measured thrust of finger-to-key produced the same level of dynamics. Now, with semi-weighted and an 88-key-weighted hammer action, a soft touch produces a soft tone and a heavier touch a louder tone.

It's up to you to decide what best suits your lifestyle. If you have the means and accommodations for an acoustic piano, you now know what to look for. If your choice is electronic, there's a wide selection from which to choose. Both would be great if you can manage it, especially if your household is active and everyone favors the room accommodating the piano. "Lucky you" can easily escape to a quiet area and play your heart out on your digital. Perfect!

6

How to Write a Simple Song

Have you ever been haunted by a tune in your head or a lyric that won't leave you alone? You want so much to turn it into a song but don't know how. You discern that for every song that's achieved recognition, there are dozens tucked away in some dusty bookcase. You also know that to write a song, then have it published and recorded by a well-known artist, is a dream few achieve. To receive royalties on it is the ultimate.

What is the origin of a song? Where does it start? Like all things that eventually turn into reality, it starts with *a simple thought—an idea*. This is one of man's greatest gifts. Thoughts appear out of the blue and must be captured on paper or tape before vanishing into thin air. With a song, that idea or concept could present itself either melodically or lyrically, sometimes both. Whichever comes first, it has to be established and developed. Everyday conversation includes clichés and phrases that can be turned into *lyrical hooks*. An idea I had for an original song called "You Said It" came while washing the dishes. I heard the phrase on television, and with wet hands, I scribbled it on some paper toweling. Later as I concentrated on the title, the *musical hook* emerged. Many others find a similar associative process: coming up with a line of lyric often suggests a melody, as well as the reverse. It starts with that initial thought.

Making melody flow effortlessly from the head to an instrument or manuscript pad is a God-given talent possessed by few. Great masters like Mozart and Beethoven had this incredible gift and wrote massive operas, symphonies, and concertos. Mozart, who was almost blinded by improper lighting while writing orchestral scores, left an enormous legacy at age thirty-five. Beethoven wrote his greatest compositions while deaf. In America, treasures left by Irving Berlin, George Gershwin, Cole Porter, Richard Rodgers, Duke Ellington, Johnny Mercer, Jerome Kern, Duke Ellington, Lerner and Lowe remain in the standard repertoire and continue to be performed worldwide. That kind of talent is overwhelming and extraordinary. But more often than not, hit songs are written by people *not* that gifted. You don't have to be a musical genius to implement the tools of the trade and turn it into a songwriting craft.

THE BASICS OF SONGWRITING

When you first learned how to play the piano, you had to learn theory. Now you can apply this information as you put your song on manuscript (paper that contains musical staves made up of five lines and four spaces.) Your song will be written out in the form of a *lead sheet* containing melody line, lyrics and chord symbols. When a song is sent to a publisher, this is how it appears. Leaf through any of the "fake books" for examples of what a lead sheet looks like. Once accepted for publication, chord symbols are transcribed into music notes and embellished with fill-ins, dynamic and interpretational markings. Take any song from a fake book and compare it to its printed sheet-music counterpart to see what the transformation entails.

When you learned how to read music, the notes, signatures, sharps, flats, rests, etc. were printed for you. Now the table is turned. *You* must print them in *your* song. You will be able to do this with your knowledge of theory.

Every professional person has years of training before going into private practice. An artist cannot paint until all supplies are assembled around the easel. A cake cannot be baked until the ingredients are gathered and portions precisely measured. So with the songwriter. In general, the basics of theory must be learned before you can create a "lead sheet." I say "in general" because there are a few remarkable exceptions. Irving Berlin could only play in one key, and had a piano specially constructed so that he could, with the flick of a control, make the piano change keys for him. Lionel Bart, best known for creating the musical *Oliver,* couldn't read music at all. He communicated his ideas through song, humming, and picking out tunes on the keyboard to various arrangers and orchestrators who then translated those ideas into readable music. But these are the exceptions.

Songwriting is a craft with rules that are basically relaxed and not carved in stone. Here are the guidelines with a fundamental explanation:

HOOKS: Hooks are lyrical and musical phrases that immediately grasp the listener's attention and become indelible through skillful repetition. The *lyrical* hook is usually the song's title because it concisely relays the story. If the hook comes to you before the story and is potent enough, the story will unfold easily. It works the other way, too. By jotting down story ideas at random, a strong title eventually emerges. To set the scene, use the title in the first line of the song and intersperse it throughout. It must be a strong, fresh idea because a title can make or break a song much as the last pitch of a tied ballgame decides the winner.

Don't let good ideas get away. Always have a pen and pad handy to jot down thoughts before they disappear forever. My song title "Don't Ask" came as I was on my way home from the supermarket. I heard that response from someone in a group behind me and wrote it down on the grocery bag. A story soon evolved, and the title became both the lyrical and the musical hook.

Titles come about in many ways. Here are some avenues to explore:

- Peruse newspaper and magazine headlines for stories on current events and trends.
- Randomly select a noun from a dictionary or thesaurus and combine it with colorful adjectives.
- Play with brand names on packages in supermarkets.
- Dally with street signs and messages on billboards.
- Look into characters and nicknames, dates and places, activities and situations.

The door is wide open to imagery, but closed to overexposed phrases like "I Love You" that have experienced burnout. Meditation and conversation are excellent sources for ideas. Who knows! You could be waiting in the wings harboring the next song in the top ten.

MUSICAL HOOKS are rhythmic or melodic phrases played *with* the lyrical hook or separately. It's the musical idea that gives the song its impetus. Take the familiar Christmas song, "Rudolph the Red-Nosed Reindeer." The song starts with both hooks appearing simultaneously, but the musical hook *singly* repeats three more times within the first 16 bars with different lyrics each time. For instance: the second repetition has the phrase "and if you ever saw it," the third is "all of the other reindeer," and the fourth is "they never let poor Rudolph." Simply put, the hook is the two-measured pattern that is visible throughout this song.

Further on, you will see lead-sheet printouts of three original songs that feature hooks. They are: "Don't Ask," "Go On Home Boy," and "Angel It's Time." Notice how they differ in format from "Rudolph the Red-Nosed Reindeer." "Rudolph" has a two-*measure* hook—"Don't Ask" has a two-*note* hook, and both "Go On Home Boy" and "Angel It's Time" have four-note patterns overlapping the bar line. Examine songs you know for patterns, and you will find quite an array. In instrumental music, there are a variety of instruments from which to choose. The musical hook could be a simple base line, a guitar riff, or a drum pattern.

STRUCTURE: Songs, like buildings, are structured, with sections consisting of *verse, chorus, bridge,* and *break.* Some are interchangeable, but the *verse* launches the song and precedes the chorus. The lyrics differ from those of the chorus because the prime function of the verse is to initiate and set up the story. The *chorus,* or "refrain," is the main section of a song and generally includes the title or hook. This is the section that is normally repeated. The *bridge* is the link between two sections and differs in melody, lyrics and harmony. It is also known as the "release." The *break* is frequently an instrumental "relief" before returning to some section of the tune.

Not a segment, but a component nonetheless, is the introduction and coda. The *introduction,* a/k/a *intro,* sets the mood and rhythm for the tune. It is played instrumentally with the length being anywhere between two to eight bars. The *coda,* a/k/a *tag,* is a passage tagged onto the end of a song to produce a more satisfying close. It may also be used as a "fade-out." Lengthwise, the coda has more liberty than the intro and occasionally does fade to a whisper before being cut off.

The sections of the original songs that follow will be identified by letters that look like a kind of shorthand code. They're used to separate the sections into verse, chorus and bridge. A repeated letter denotes a repeated section. For example: *AABA* as seen in "Angel It's Time" and "Perhaps" merely acknowledges that the song's format is A(chorus) A(chorus) B(verse) A (chorus.) Before 1960, according to the book *Songwriting* by Stephen Citron, *A* was always the chorus and *B* always the verse. Rules have apparently relaxed, and now whatever section appears first is assumed as *A. ABAB,* characterized in "Go On Home Boy," signifies that the breakdown is A(verse) B(chorus)

A(verse) B(chorus). *AAB/AAB,* the format for "Don't Ask" is simply A(verse) A(verse) B(chorus) and a repetition of same. "Case Dismissed" has three verses, each consisting of 16 bars. The first eight bars are repeated, thereby making the format *AA.* *ABABCB* is another code that indicates that the usual verse/chorus/verse/chorus has inserted a bridge (C) prior to returning to the preceding section.

Understanding hooks and structure and the major roles they play in songwriting now makes what seemed like an impossible dream within reach.

RANGE AND LENGTH: The key to successful songwriting is keeping the melody simple and within a singable range. That span is approximately an octave and a half. Remember, not every singer has an extended range like Barbra Streisand and Cleo Laine. They have top arrangers create special charts for them that rely on modulation and other effects to compensate for their exceptional voices. But initially, play it safe and stick with the tried and true. Let the pros handle the rest.

As to the length of a song, if you're starting to go beyond three minutes, you're headed for trouble. Have you ever listened to a speaker or an entertainer and found yourself squirming in your seat? The obvious reason is that he/she overstayed his/her welcome. Say what you have to say and stop. The arrangement, with an intro and tag, will extend the playing time a bit, so stay within the safety zone.

MELODY: A melody that flows in an effortless direction plus phrases that build on preceding phrases are known as *musical direction.* Phrases and ideas must be kept to a minimum because it's simplicity that defines the line between holding a listener or losing him. Hit songs, both past and present, will prove this to be true every time. Staying power comes from repetition; it's a chant that becomes imbedded in the mind.

Are you ready to try your hand at melody writing? Start by

selecting a favorite tune and *substitute* some of the written notes in the melody line with notes of your choice. It's a bold move and one you didn't anticipate, but it is a step in the right direction. Make notations on the score of your alternative notes, and when you're finished, play the original and then the substitute. If it's not to your liking, keep at it until you come up with something that sounds fitting.

Another idea is to try creating a tune by using the numbers on your credit card, old lottery tickets, cell/home phone numbers and area/zip codes—any combination that comes to mind. Example: Pick a telephone number at random: 462-4315. In the Key of C (with C as number 1), transfer these numbers to correlate with the letters of the piano keys (462-4315 is F A D F E C G). Write these down on manuscript paper, making each letter a quarter note. (See Illustration #1.) Play it several times until it feels comfortable. Count out the time and it can easily be a 4/4 time signature. Insert a G-clef and 4/4 meter and you have your first try in print. Now, *change* the time value of these notes. Instead of all quarter notes, alternate between a *half* note and a quarter note. (See Illustration #2.) This time it works out to be three beats to a measure. Insert the G-clef and 3/4 time signature, and you have your *first variation.* One more time—write it out alternating between a *quarter* and a half note. Again, three beats to a measure and a *second variation.* (See Illustration #3.)

By taking a telephone number and interpolating it, you become aware of how free you are in writing music. If you don't like the order of the numbers and decide to alter one or two, no problem. Keep in mind that a scale contains seven letters/numbers with 8 and 9 being duplicates of 1 and 2 (an octave higher). Zero is of no value, but do incorporate 8 and 9. They're within the recommended singing range of an octave and a half. Play each illustration and be aware of how a simple change like time/ note value alters the mood significantly. The first was somber and the latter two more rhythmic and singable. Music is actually a blend of melody and rhythm. Mozart created some of his greatest masterpieces by rolling dice. It's worth a try.

Now play the identical notes in each illustration, but change the *key signatures* of #2 and #3. (Can you see why knowledge of theory is imperative?) Illustration #1 will remain as is. Change #2 into the key of D by adding two sharps and #3 into the key of E-flat by inserting three flats. Repeat them several times, and you can readily hear how incidentals (sharps, flats and naturals) come into play. It's absolutely mind-boggling what can be done with just twelve notes. All the music ever written, from pop to classical, is a simple combination of melody, rhythm, harmony and twelve tones.

Before touching on how to get your own melody on paper, be adventurous and try writing a melody to existing lyrics. You will be forced to comply with the rhythm and flow of words as well as the phrasing. Observing the already assigned harmonic progressions and rhythmic patterns is the best way to hear what fits and what doesn't. Having access to a digital piano with a rhythm section will allow you to experiment with the style of your melody. At the touch of a button, you can change the rhythm from ballad to rock, from country to Latin, etc. This is not wasting time. This is an ongoing lesson, and you're constantly learning.

The easiest way to get your own tune on manuscript is to sing it on tape and have someone transcribe it for you. If you recall, that route was taken by Irving Berlin and Lionel Bart. Before you ask for help, see if you are able to sing each note and find the corresponding key on the piano; then write it down on staff paper. This will be a rough draft because you must then figure out key and time signatures, note values, etc. Don't fret, though. Even if you flounder, there is always someone who will come to your rescue. Ask an experienced musician or teacher to help you. They will gladly show you how to beat out time to enable you to correctly evaluate each note. Rests and bar lines, as well as sharps and flats, will take their proper places and a time and key signature will become established.

Lyrics: In lyric writing, the idea being conveyed must remain simple and contained. Like an octopus with a body and eight tentacles, the idea should stay within the body and not get carried away in eight different directions. Before you start to write, assemble all the "tools" you will need. Develop pictures about the chosen subject and jot down these ideas as they emerge. List all related information and conditions and question their connection. Keep what works and eliminate the rest. When finished, put these ideas in sequence so they're at your disposal and accessible. From all of this data, a musical hook or song title may emerge. If not, there's no rush. Use a "working title" until something occurs that "says it all." Remember, a strong title is pivotal. It alone can make or break a song.

It's extremely difficult to write anything of substance without a thesaurus and a good dictionary by your side. They are my collaborators regardless of what I write. They're also a *must* for spelling accuracy. For lyric writing, add a dictionary of synonyms and antonyms and a rhyming dictionary to that stack. You will soon find out how indispensable they are.

Every profession seems to have its own jargon. Have you ever listened to a group of doctors or lawyers engaged in "shop talk?" You couldn't eavesdrop if you wanted to, their lingo is so foreign to the outsider. The same holds true for songwriters. Here are some of the terms with definitions and examples that you will encounter along the way.

- *alliteration:* a repetition of the same first letter (usually a consonant) in a group of words (e.g., the sun sank slowly).

- *allusion:* an indirect or casual reference to someone or something (e.g., He made allusions to recent events without recounting them).
- *assonance:* a substitute for rhyme in which the vowels are repeated but the consonants are different (e.g., brave—vain, lone—show).
- *imagery:* descriptions and figures of speech that help the mind form forceful or beautiful pictures (e.g., the girl's blue dress with the white bows and brass buttons).
- *metaphor:* a figure of speech in which a word denoting one idea is used in place of another to suggest a likeness between them. Metaphors and similes and analogies all make comparisons, but the three figures differ in form and fullness. An *analogy* is usually a rather full comparison, showing or implying several points of similarity. A *simile* makes the comparison exact and labels it by the introductory word "like" or "as" (e.g., a face like marble; as brave as a lion). A *metaphor* is the shortest, most compact of these comparisons. In it, the likeness is implied rather than stated explicitly (e.g., a copper sky; a heart of stone).

With all of this at your beck and call, your ear is still the most reliable source of all and will distinctly tell you when a word doesn't fit. Don't force it. Rephrase the line or go to your reference books for help. The key words are all there. Learning to synchronize words with melody and rhythm is an obvious essential. If you emphasize the wrong syllable or force a rhyme, it will stick out like a sore thumb. Sing it, however crudely, whenever you have difficulty with a phrase. It's the natural guide to ascertaining the curve of a line. You can be sure your ear will tell you the truth. There are songs that don't need to rhyme as long as they "sing" well. Words and music should come across feeling fused and integrated, not coerced. In other words, *songwriting is a wedding of words and music.* Use only recognizable words and make sure phrases are easily understood. This is no time to show off your extensive vocabulary. Lyrics have to make sense and paint a clear picture. Insert comparisons for a more creative and accurate image. Also, continue to write down ideas as they pop out of the blue. Explosions of creativity are the spontaneous thoughts that must be captured before they evaporate. You can always insert this material or replace parts of the song with it before it's finalized.

I must emphasize how important repetition is to a song. Children remember nursery rhymes because of reiteration and rhyme. So do adults. Write in the "now" and keep phrases conversational, colorful, and singable by changing nouns and adjectives. Be wary of the temptation to use clichés and trite phrases. They have been worn to a frazzle. When writing something with a beat, a drum machine played softly in the background will help. Try mixing meters to draw attention. The verse could be in 4/4 and the chorus in 3/4. It also does *not* matter which comes first—the music or the words. Either way, the first segment written sets the mood, and the second will fall in place. Just go with the flow. Take a break if you start to get tired. Only a refreshed mind can lift blocks and allow fresh ideas to flow. If you're hung up on a section but know the basic concept, leave it alone and go to another section. You can fill that in later.

Songs are more personalized when written alone, but finding a collaborator may be to your advantage. Whether your partner handles the words or the music, you'll soon know if this relationship is going to work. If flexibility and compatibility are there from the start, it's a good sign. Partners must be accommodating and recognize when compromise is needed. A songwriter most often searches for someone who is proficient in an area where he or she is deficient. It's a smart move and can bring both writers benefit. A co-writer can add that new dimension and energy to an idea that was stymied up until now. That feedback might have been the tonic needed to make words and music work in sync.

If the relationship doesn't work for whatever reason, ask your mentor or an experienced writer for references. Be open to fresh ideas and new contacts. You don't want your creativity to be squashed. At this point, checking out songwriting seminars and classes may not be a bad idea. Contact music and English departments at universities and local colleges for possible collaborators. There is someone out there who will fill that void. Just keep trying.

As for teaching videos for the novice songwriter, my sources are unaware of any available in today's market. However, there are excellent books for the first-time music writer and lyricist. Before placing an order, speak with someone qualified to ensure you are requesting the right book for your needs. At the same time, ask to be put on their mailing list. By doing so, you'll be up-to-date with new arrivals. For books and publishers, see Appendix I.

Most of these books can be ordered through the publisher or purchased in major book stores like Barnes & Noble and Borders. Check your local library, but libraries affiliated with major music schools and universities and music complexes like Lincoln Center in New York City are more apt to have them.

ILLUSTRATIONS

Using published works other than mine to show *how* and *where* to use songwriting basics is a violation of the copyright law. Therefore, I selected five original songs for that purpose. A glossary will visually link the terms to illustrations. First, though, a brief rundown on each song.

"Angel It's Time" I collaborated with a lyricist on this novelty number. The story came first, so I "doctored" it to conform to the natural rhythmic pulse that was developing. As it turned out, the song had both a musical hook and a lyrical hook. Both hooks start the song and remain prominent throughout. The musical *and* lyrical hook appear together twice. The structure is AABA—chorus, chorus, bridge, and chorus. The melody is rather subdued so as not to interfere with the story, the song's focal point. I created an arrangement of this song for my vocal and instrumental trio (shown in the next chapter). It has a strong jazz/rock beat backing it up. (The song was written on the Long Island Railroad on a trip home to see my mom.)

"Perhaps" It's a ballad with an AABA form—three choruses and a release. I wrote both the words and music to a story based on a broken romance. The melody came first and was written on a subway ride that took twenty minutes. The lyrics followed later and were put to paper with "yours truly" comfortably propped up in bed. The title became the first word of the song. This lyrical hook appears three times during the song—twice in the first section A. With the story being of the essence, the melody was tempered in order to comply with the poetic flow. "Perhaps" clearly defines musical direction and is a good example of how a melody builds within a series of phrases, giving the song direction and continuity. It resembles a kite floating in the sky on a breezy day.

"Go On Home Boy" One evening, I overheard this idiom repeated several times at a nearby table in a restaurant. It turned out to be a group of chums pleading with a buddy to go home and "try again." This idiom became the title and lyrical hook as well as the musical hook. This simple country-western is long-winded and needed subdued music to keep up with the patter. The ABAB structure is verse, chorus, verse, chorus with the title appearing only in the chorus. The same rhythmic pattern accompanies the title each time.

In reading the finished story, my fingers started to tap to the pulse of each line. I started picturing an audience "thigh slapping" to an energetic rhythmic guitarist perched on a bar stool singing at the top of his lungs. This inspired me to write a peppy arrangement for a demo record. (Yes, the male vocalist *was* backed by that energetic guitarist and ensemble.)

"Don't Ask" This is the phrase I overheard as I walked home with a bag of groceries. It eventually became the musical *and* lyrical hook. "Don't Ask" is another long-winded, toe-tapping, rock/country song with an AAB-AAB form. A rhythmic pattern that is repetitious concurs with the hooks. The two notes of the musical hook overlap the bar line and becomes anticipatory rather quickly. This song's arrangement for a demo record featured a male vocalist backed by a rhythm ensemble. "Demos" are addressed in the next chapter.

"Case Dismissed" This story about a defendant pleading with the judge for mercy had no choice but to be long-winded. Certainly any competition from the melody would detract from the tale being told. This story is told in three verses and has a "loose" AA form. A lyricist collaborated with me, and an arrangement is written out in the following chapter.

The glossary below identifies and links the fundamental sections of the following five songs.

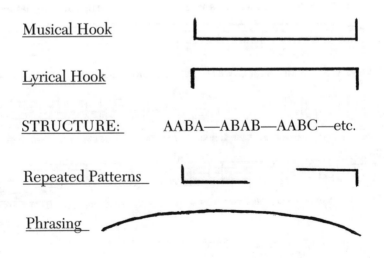

Musical Hook	
Lyrical Hook	
STRUCTURE:	AABA—ABAB—AABC—etc.
Repeated Patterns	
Phrasing	

ANGEL IT'S TIME

© 1968 JOAN ST JAMES & LEONARD DALEY

PERHAPS

A PER-HAPS I'VE LEARNED A LESSON—ALL LOVE AF-FAIRS HAVE TO END— I THOUGHT PER-

HAPS I COULD BE WITH YOU—WHILE I SEARCHED FOR WAYS TO MAKE A-MENDS—THE

A HOUR WAS FAST AP-PROACH-ING—THIS LOVE AF-FAIR NEARED ITS END— HOW COULD I

FACE UP TO TELLING YOU—WE MUST PART AND NE-VER LOVE A-GAIN——— YOU

B HEARD I BE-LONGED TO AN-O-THER— A TALE YOU RE-FUSED TO BE-LIEVE— I

CAUSED YOU SUCH PAIN WHEN I SAID IT WAS TRUE—SUCH PAIN ILL TRY HARD TO UN-DO—PER-

A HAPS THERE LIES AN AN-SWER—I'LL SEARCH 'TIL I FIND A WAY— A

LOVE LIKE OURS IS TOO STRONG TO FADE AND DIE—TRUST IN LOVE AND WE'LL FIND A WAY.

© 1969   JOAN ST. JAMES AND LEONARD DALEY

© 1976 JOAN ST. JAMES

DON'T ASK

CASE DISMISSED

© 1969   JOHN ST. JAMES AND LEONARD DALEY

General sources, including biographies and autobiographies of songwriting legends like Larry Hart, Johnny Mercer, Oscar Hammerstein, Richard Rodgers, Jerome Kern, George and Ira Gershwin, Cole Porter, Richard Whiting, Frank Loesser and Stephen Sondheim can be immeasurably helpful. These writers will give you the "bigger picture" through *their* discussion of various songwriting techniques. While this may seem almost too advanced for you, you'll see that once you've mastered some theoretical basics, you can begin exploring the fascinating world of songwriting almost immediately. With a combination of hands-on instruction and a list of excellent resources, which will complement this instruction, you may well be on your way to wowing folks with an original song at your next party.

My first exposure to structure and style came in a required course at Juilliard called *Literature and Materials of Music*. I was asked to play "September Song" by Kurt Weill in its entirety for the class and then in sections for "dissection." It was easy to recognize the AABA structure. Rodgers and Hammerstein's musical *Carousel,* contains two lovely ballads—"If I Loved You" and "You'll Never Walk Alone." Listen to or play "If I Loved You" and the standard AABA layout is evident. Do the same with "You'll Never Walk Alone," and you will notice there really is *no* structure. It starts and builds in momentum and intensity and reaches its pinnacle just before ending. This simply points out how much freedom there is in writing music. There is a format, but you're *not limited* to that format. Earlier I wrote that songwriting is a craft with relaxed rules. "You'll Never Walk Alone" proves just that. But then, Richard Rodgers was a born genius and a prolific writer. If you study the writing and styles of the musical giants, you will begin to understand the freedom of expression. Formats lay a foundation but creativity has no boundary. You can almost go anywhere with a song if you have an unlimited imagination.

With regard to style, look at the difference in writing when

Richard Rodgers wrote with lyricist Larry Hart. Witty phrases and humorous words are synonymous with Rodgers and Hart, whereas Rodgers and Hammerstein were more majestic and serious in tone. George Gershwin's writing is discernible through his advanced harmonies and jazz influence. Cole Porter's rhythmic patterns plus brilliant lyrics made him a legend. The Beatles put themselves on the map showing their unique style in songs like "Yesterday," "Something" and "Hey Jude."

I know this is advanced material, but this is the only way to make progress. You are absorbing this whether you know it or not. Spend time going through literature and analyze the approaches taken by various writers. You will develop a much clearer insight into songwriting. Since fake books are loaded with material and concise in approach, this would be a good way to start. Remember, as you listen and learn and compare notes, your subconscious mind is storing more than you realize. You will find yourself starting to incorporate these ideas into your own songs.

7

How to Write a Simple Arrangement

The term "musical arrangement" is intimidating to the novice. At the beginning, it frightened me, too. Only when I was told to compare a song to the basic black dress in every woman's wardrobe did it fall into perspective. Accessories are needed to enhance and complete the outfit and are chosen from an array of belts, jewelry, scarves, shoes, and handbags. Just as the dress *needs* the accessories, so does a song *need* an arrangement. A song takes on an arrangement when sections are added to it, such as an *introduction* (a/k/a *intro*), *fill-ins, breaks,* and *endings* (a/k/a *tag.*) You played them without realizing it when learning how to read sheet music. They were already added. As youngsters, we started listening to recordings and took the ensemble backing a vocalist for granted. We assumed that's the way the song was written. Little did we know that without the arrangement, that song might have wound up like many other songs—collecting dust on a bookshelf.

How many arrangers, like songwriters past and present, possess the magic to turn out hit after hit after hit? Listen to the recordings of Frank Sinatra, Tony Bennett, Ella Fitzgerald, Rosemary Clooney, and their peers and you will realize it was the incredible talent of arrangers like Don Costa, Axel Stordahl,

Gordon Jenkins, Billy May and Nelson Riddle that put their songs into our national archives. Without their expertise, the song might have taken the path to oblivion.

Musical arrangements—just like songs—run the gamut from simple to intricate. It is important to remember that the *song* is being sold—*not* the arrangement. A good arrangement is meant to *enhance* a song, not get in its way. Working alone and with small groups throughout my career taught me many lessons about arranging material to set it off optimally. The best route is usually the simplest. Adding just a bit of ad-lib (freedom with tempo) and relying on key changes, plus interspersing voice with instrumental music, will add color, avoid monotony, and keep the outline clean.

Once you've written your first song on a lead sheet, you're ready to learn how to "set it" or "present it" in a simple arrangement. This is not as daunting a task as you may fear. Whether you know it or not, you already arranged it subconsciously when you first played it and heard the chords and embellishments in your head.

Let me re-introduce one of my own songs called "Case Dismissed." This song was arranged for a demonstration tape (a/k/a demo) by backing the vocalist with a rock beat provided by my trio of piano, bass and drums. Since this song is a novelty with emphasis on lyrics, the background music remained subdued. Whether a vocalist is accompanied by an ensemble or solo pianist, the basic arrangement stays the same. Even if other instruments are added later on, all one has to do is write out those parts and leave the arrangement as is. Any addition is considered an embellishment.

Go to Illustration #1 ("Case Dismissed") and observe the two-bar pattern that serves as the intro, fill-in and tag:

- The *intro* preceding the first chorus uses this two-bar pattern four times, making the introduction eight bars in length.

- The *fill-ins* are played as indicated between choruses.
- The *tag* is a duplicate of the intro.

It's fascinating to see how one pattern applied in three different ways can *tie* a song together so easily.

Another technique used frequently in arranging is *modulation* (a change of keys). The lead sheet for "Case Dismissed" is written entirely in D-minor (see illustration #1, page 96). By modulating *the last two bars of both fill-ins* to introduce a new key to the following chorus, intensity and excitement as well as color are brought to the arrangement (see illustration #2, page 97). Simply put: *fill-in #1* goes from D-minor to E-flat minor to set Verse #2 in E-flat minor. *Fill-in #2* goes from E-flat minor to E-minor to set Verse #3 and tag in E-minor.

CASE DISMISSED

CASE DISMISSED

© 1969 JOAN ST. JAMES AND LEONARD DALEY

Let's take another song from the previous chapter and analyze the arrangement. "Angel It's Time" is a totally different arrangement from "Case Dismissed." This was vocally and instrumentally designed for the all-girl trio and started with the bass and drums playing a four-bar rhythmic pattern.

The illustration on page 98 shows a sketch of this pattern followed by a vocal introduction (sung on syllable *AH*). The song is in three-part harmony with the rhythmic pattern changing to an easy swing at the release. The first half of the second chorus was an instrumental jazz improvisation. The voices picked up at the release and modulated up a half-tone for the last 16 bars. The 12-measure tag repeats the lyrical/musical hook five times, bringing the song to a dramatic close. (The modulation is optional and not written out in this illustration.)

DEMO TAPES

The explicit purpose of a demo tape is to *show* your song— *not* to instruct how it's to be performed. Submit a lead sheet and a tape of the arranged song to the A & R (artist and repertoire) department of a record studio. Your song is copyrighted the instant it is written. To indicate this, place a c within a circle (©), the year, and name(s) at the bottom of your lead sheet. That's it! If the song is accepted by a publisher, register it with the Library

ANGEL IT'S TIME

of Congress Copyright Office, 101 Independence Ave. S.E., Washington, D.C. 20559-6000. Royalties are received for recordings manufactured and distributed and for performances on radio and TV. Some of the terms affiliated with this process are:

- *copyright*—shows ownership of song and legal protection
- *cut*—to record (to cut a record)
- *demo*—not for release, for "show" purpose only
- *pitch*—an attempt to interest an artist or producer into recording a song

Another option is to have your demo made in a studio. That's what I did. A reputable studio and a good technician are invaluable in achieving a balance level, doing retakes, and completing the master tape. You want the best tape possible, so don't be skimpy when reserving studio time. This is no time for penny-pinching. Once the session is over, get a supply of cassettes and keep the master tape in case you need extra copies. A good demo tape could lead to a signed contract and a profitable writing career. For more information on demos, see Appendix J.

You should really take time out to pat yourself on the back for what you've already accomplished. That hidden dream to play the piano *has* become a reality; otherwise, you wouldn't be reading about arranging right now. Your love of music brought you to the point where sight-reading is no longer a challenge. You're ready to try *your* hand at creating. To help with this, there is a sequence of books by Marvin Kahn that is by far the easiest to follow for students of piano. I strongly suggest that you buy the set and study them in sequence. The instruction is explicit with illustrations and exercises covering aspects including but not limited to the following:

- syncopation
- broken tenths
- waltz and swing bass and western-style bass

- breaks and fill-ins
- harmonization and transposition
- embellishments and improvisation
- introductions and endings
- use of the pedal
- arpeggios and close positions

For books and publishers, see Appendix K.

Take your time going through these volumes. Practice and memorize the illustrations and use them where applicable in the standard repertoire. Some will fit, some won't. Try new phrases on the same tunes, and you will eventually get the knack. As you advance, play the intros and fill-ins written on sheet music and try embellishing them. Go one step further and write your own intro and fill-ins around the given chord. Become even more creative by mixing and interchanging all the ideas already tried. You will begin to feel more and more confident as all falls into place. Don't be frustrated if at first the results are slow. Nothing worthwhile comes easily. My only caution to you is to follow the "stepladder" approach. *One step at a time!* Don't move up until you feel comfortable at that level. You will be using all this material sooner or later; therefore, learn it thoroughly.

Continue to train your ear by listening to the arrangements of musical giants. Pay special attention to their *style*. Unfortunately, the northeast region of the United States doesn't have a radio station at this time that exclusively plays standards from the American Songbook. The last bastion featured the well-known musicologist and radio personality, Jonathan Schwartz, son of legendary songwriter Arthur Schwartz. Besides playing notable songs, Jonathan had a format that educated the audience at the same time. For example, he played the "Frank Sinatra Sings Johnny Mercer" songbook in its entirety and then repeated those songs sung once again by Sinatra with different arrangements. His intention was to demonstrate how a song varies in mood and character when arranged by another creative mind. He made his listeners aware that by changing tempo, rhythm, harmony and instrumentation, a song is "redesigned," giving it a brand-new sound, intensity and style. He enlightened the audience further by selecting *one* song followed by several vocal renditions of it. Each stylist was so distinctive in interpretation that one had to be consciously aware it was the same song. What a masterful musical education! Jonathan is currently the artistic director of New York's Lincoln Center American Songbook Series and has a program on radio station WNYC-AM.

FINE-TUNING YOUR SKILLS

Remember—you're *subconsciously absorbing* all you hear. The "stop" and "rewind" features of tape players are ideal to jot down ideas the way you did when you wrote your first song. Continue listening to orchestral scores behind singers as well as big-band charts. What you assumed once to be monumental and out of reach now makes sense. All you have to do is apply yourself.

The best way to tie these segments together is to engage an experienced musician and work with that person one-on-one. There must be graduate students in conservatories and universities who would love to give you the benefit of their burgeoning minds and usually at a more-than-affordable price. The ideal person is the musician who makes a living doing this.

In my Juilliard days, I had a pianist/arranger come to the school once a week to help me out. He took one tune at a time, played it several different ways by changing harmony, rhythm, fill-ins, and intros, and taped it for study and future reference. I learned how rhythmic patterns and modulation create the color and style we crave. Years later, when I got my first job with my new trio playing music for ballroom dancing, my drummer taught me authentic Latin American rhythms and my bassist taught me how to play "montunos"—a Latin-style improvisation around one or two chords. Both were responsible for widening my musical repertory. You *can reach* the level of proficiency you strived so hard to attain. Create a new goal and cross that *fine line* between remaining an amateur and becoming a professional.

MEDLEY

Now it's time to forge ahead, put all your skills to work, and reap the rewards. Before we get to the *real* reward, let me explain how to put together a *medley* of songs using simple modulation. The word "medley" is defined as a mixture, mingling, variety, miscellany, or diversity. *Roget's Thesaurus* adds hodgepodge, melange, jumble and assemblage to an already long list. The music world's definition of a medley is "a group of songs played without interruption." In other words, a performer "segues" from one song to another without stopping. When a musician is asked to play "some Cole Porter" or "some tunes from Andrew Lloyd Weber's *Phantom of the Opera,"* the request is for a selection of tunes from that composer or show. The following guidelines should give you an idea as to how to put together your own medley of choice.

- an "intro" is played only before the opening song
- each succeeding song should be in a different key
- vary the mood/tempo between tunes
- select songs from the musical score of a show—no need to play them all
- a medley can be any length you wish
- eliminate the refrain that precedes the chorus unless it is pertinent to the song
- changing the meter *within* a song can be effective—for in-

stance, a waltz in 3/4 time can switch to 4/4 at the release and revert to 3/4 for the last eight measures

- interchange tempo with ad-lib
- a radical change in style between two songs in the same key may not need a modulation
- modulate within a song if there is a natural opening
- use the piano's upper register for color—e.g., a tinkling music box, bells or chimes
- close a medley with an "attention-getter"—a song bright in tempo, dramatic, or a fragment of the theme song

In putting this together, remember that music is *audible* and its purpose is to provide listening pleasure to the audience. That's why playing a series of slow songs in sequence in the same key can be monotonous and drab. Use modulation to distinguish one from the other. Always apply "audible" color to music just as an artist uses color to illuminate a painting. Whether it's a group of songs by an individual composer, show tunes, songs of an ethnic culture, or hymns, "shift gears" whenever possible. It not only holds the attention of an audience, it gives leeway to create. (See Appendix L.)

Use this concept to put together a medley of songs or fragments of songs with similar tunes to create a sort of "musical play." Try juxtaposing "The Lady Is a Tramp" with "Luck Be a Lady Tonight" and "The Lady's in Love With You." By using the word *lady* as the connecting theme, the audience's perception of each song is altered as they hear them in this setting.

To explain how to use a *fragment* of a song, I did just that in a medley from the Rodgers and Hammerstein show, *Oklahoma*. I opened the medley with an *intro* and played the entire title song. Several tunes from that show followed, and the medley ended with only the *last 8 bars* (or fragment) of the title song plus a tag.

There is no *time frame, minimum,* or *maximum* in a medley. If I'm asked to play "some Gershwin," for instance, there is plenty from which to choose. Always included, however, is the main theme of the perennial favorite, "Rhapsody in Blue." Illustrations appear shortly that depict how themes can be "lifted" from classical compositions like concertos, symphonies, suites, sonatas, and operas and embodied in a medley. As heretical as it may sound to some purists, you *can* take a well-known classical piece and single out a melodic section, add lyrics to it, arrange it, and put it on the charts. Singer Perry Como did just that with two popular Chopin piano compositions—"Till the End of Time," lifted from the *Polonaise in A-Flat,* and "I'm Always Chasing Rainbows" from the *Fantaisie Impromptu* were huge sellers. Frank Sinatra's immense library of recordings includes themes extracted from Tschaikowsky and Rachmaninoff. Della Reese's recording of "Don't You Know" was lifted right out of Puccini's opera, *La Boheme.* Opera fans know it as "Muzetta's Waltz."

The enormous success of The Three Tenors (Luciano Pavarotti, Placido Domingo and José Carreras) made the operatic aria "the new kid on the block." I stopped in my tracks when I heard "Nessun Dorma" from Puccini's *Turandot* sung by a rock artist.

This might seem like too much heresy even to consider, but remember that many orchestral arrangers have set favorite classics in new forms. Leopold Stokowski, in particular, reset many of Bach's organ pieces in splendidly lush orchestral arrangements. J. S. Bach, who delighted in musical innovation, might himself have applauded this.

Earlier, I mentioned that only the main theme of the "Rhapsody in Blue" is played in my Gershwin medley. There is a simple explanation for this. When a pianist is preparing to perform in a concert hall and selects either the "Rhapsody in Blue" or "An American in Paris" from Gershwin's enormous library, he will have the rapt attention of the audience. They are there to hear the original composition in its entirety. It's not always so in a more relaxed atmosphere like a lounge or a cocktail gathering.

In this case, when a guest requests either of the above, he/she really expects to hear recognizable *themes*. I learned that early on, when I obliged a guest with Richard Addinsell's "Warsaw Concerto" and Richard Rodgers' "Slaughter on Tenth Avenue" only to lose him halfway through the piece. The atmosphere and environment of a social establishment is not conducive to such lengthy material. Therefore, the best way to fulfill a request of that nature is to *tie* the themes together in an abridged arrangement or medley.

EXAMPLES OF MEDLEYS

The following will illustrate *two* basic techniques: (1) simply tie songs together; (2) *lift* sections out of compositions and tie them together. The first illustration is of well-known Christmas carols that are virtually left untouched, yet fall within the aforementioned guidelines. Before playing them, observe the changes in key, meter and tempo between the three carols.

There is only one modulation and that is between "Angels We Have Heard on High" and "The First Noel." The simplest and easiest modulation here is to hold the F chord in the last measure of "Angels" as is, follow that with an *A chord* in the *root position,* hold for three beats, then proceed to the pick-up notes of "The First Noel" in tempo. The A chord is used because it is the dominant of the key of the following carol.

After playing "The First Noel," the spirited mood of "Joy to the World" requires no introduction. It makes its own statement. Play as is and stretch the last two bars to indicate the end of the medley.

"Angels We Have Heard on High," "The First Noel," and "Joy to the World" are on pages 107–110.

Angels We Have Heard on High

French Carol
Arr. by Kowalchyk/Lancaster

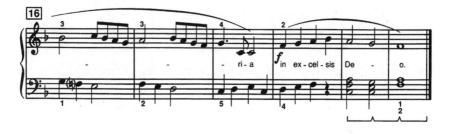

Music engraving: Nancy Butler

The First Noel

English Carol
Arr. by Kowalchyk/Lancaster

Moderato

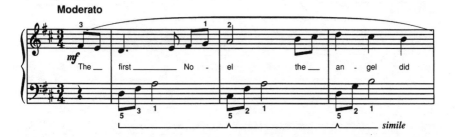

Music engraving: Nancy Butler

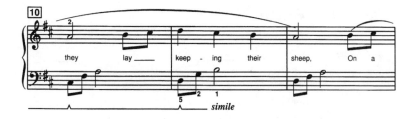

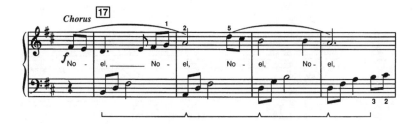

Joy to the World

George F. Handel
Arr. by Kowalchyk/Lancaster

Music engraving: Nancy Butler

The second illustration includes three popular themes taken from world-famous piano concertos; they appear in this order:

- Tschaikowsky's *First Piano Concerto*
- Mozart's *Piano Concerto No. 21*
- Rachmaninoff's *Second Piano Concerto*

When browsing through volumes of music in stores and libraries, you no doubt notice that music is arranged, transcribed and edited to satisfy every level of playing ability. The pianist's learning repertoire is completely covered from the elementary level to the most advanced. I chose the intermediate level as a "middle of the road" plateau for this sequence.

The Tschaikowsky is in *3/4* meter in the key of *C* and starts with an introduction followed by the theme from the first movement. The theme is repeated once again (measure 25) and finishes with a short extension.

The theme from the second movement of the Mozart that follows is in the key of *F* with a *4/4* meter. Since the change in pulse and mood between the two themes is apparent, my only suggestion would be for the performer to play the first measure *twice,* basically to emphasize and support that change. This also has a repetition of the theme starting at measure 14.

The Rachmaninoff, the last theme in this medley, is in the key of *C* with a *4/4* meter. You will feel like Rachmaninoff himself after you finish playing it. The change between the Mozart and Rachmaninoff is so formidable, I suggest you don't tamper with any kind of segue. Just play this beautiful melody from the third movement of the concerto as is and fantasize about playing that coda in Carnegie Hall with a symphony orchestra backing you. Talk about a glimpse of heaven!

Russian-born Peter Ilyich Tchaikovsky (1840–1893) is one of the great composers of the Romantic period. He excelled as a conductor and taught at the Moscow Conservatory, resigning in 1878 to devote himself entirely to composing. This piece was premiered in Boston in 1875 and quickly found its way into the repertoire of great pianists all over the world. Tchaikovsky composed in almost every genre and was also known for his beautiful melodies, rich harmonies, exciting rhythms, and mood contrasts.

Theme from the

First Piano Concerto

Peter Ilyich Tchaikovsky (1840–1893)
Arr. Willard A. Palmer

Wolfgang Amadeus Mozart (1756–1791) composed the *Piano Concerto No. 21* in December of 1785, when he was at the height of his popularity and financial success. This beautiful theme is taken from the slow movement of the concerto.

Theme from the

Piano Concerto No. 21

Wolfgang Amadeus Mozart
(1756–1791)
Arr. Allan Small

(a) Start the trill on E.

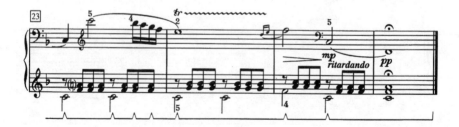

Theme from the

Second Piano Concerto

Sergei Rachmaninoff (1873–1943)
Op. 18
Arr. Allan Small

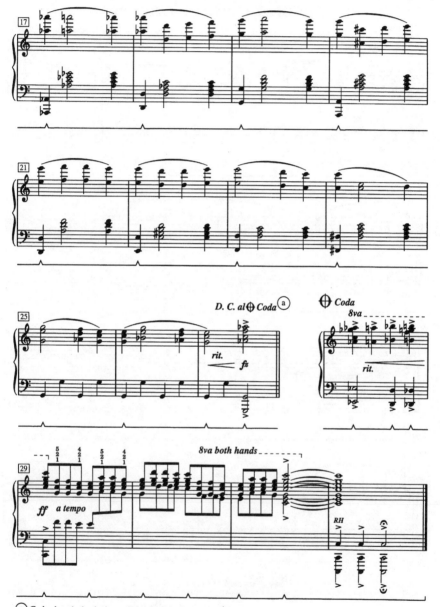

There is no end to the material from the classical repertoire that can effectively be combined into a series, such as themes from Beethoven's *Moonlight* and *Pathetique* sonatas plus his "Ode to Joy" from the *Ninth Symphony*. Take the well-known melodies from the ballads, etudes, nocturnes, preludes and waltzes of the lyrical genius, Frederick Chopin. Already mentioned were the smash recordings Perry Como had with *Polonaise in A-Flat* and *Fantaisie Impromptu*. The prodigious music of Tschaikowsky is played somewhere in the universe every day. You should have no trouble combining the themes from his Fifth and Sixth symphonies with the love theme from *Romeo and Juliet*. His *Swan Lake* ballet and The *Nutcracker Suite* are so diverse in tempo, style, and dynamics, you'd have more than enough material from which to choose.

What about opera! A great deal of the music we heard in our childhood was actually operatic arias transformed into popular music. George Bizet's *Carmen* is a perfect example. I used to parade around the house to the "Toreador Song" and dance away to the "Habanera." Giuseppi Verdi, probably the most prolific operatic composer of all time, along with Giacomo Puccini, left us with immortals like *Aida, Il Trovatore, La Traviata, Rigoletto, Otello, Macbeth,* and *Luisa Miller,* to name a few. Who doesn't recognize and respond to "Celeste Aida," "La Donna è Mobile," "The Anvil Chorus," and the "Triumphal March." Puccini's "Muzetta's Waltz" from *La Bohème,* "Vissi d'arte" from *Tosca,* and "Un Bel Di Vedremo" from *Madame Butterfly* are universally cherished. Pavarotti cannot leave the stage unless he sings "Recondita Armonia" from *Tosca,* "Che Gelida Manina" from *La Boheme,* and, of course, "Nessun Dorma" from *Turandot.*

Just for the fun of it, a printout of three of the arias mentioned follows. Play them and play *with* them until you find a suitable grouping.

Giuseppe Verdi is considered to be one of the greatest composers of opera. His first two operas were modest successes, though his personal life during this time was filled with grief; between the years 1838 and 1840, his two infant children and wife died. He continued to compose, completing *Nabucco*, his third opera, in 1842. It was a great success, and Verdi quickly became one of Italy's most popular composers. This aria, from the opera *Rigoletto*, became one of Europe's most popular melodies when it was presented in 1851.

La Donna è Mobile

from *Rigoletto*

Giuseppe Verdi (1813–1901)
Arr. Willard A. Palmer

Giacomo Puccini (1858–1924), the famous Italian opera composer, came from a very musical family. As a young man, he had primarily been a composer of sacred music. But after hearing Giuseppe Verdi's opera *Aida*, Puccini decided to become a dramatic composer. This waltz is from one of Puccini's most popular operas, called *La Bohème*, about two poor lovers living in Paris. This beautiful opera, still popular today, helped make Puccini famous around the world, and he soon became a very wealthy man.

Theme from

Musetta's Waltz

from *La Bohème*

Giacomo Puccini (1858–1924)
Arr. Willard A. Palmer

George Bizet was a childhood prodigy, having entered the Paris Conservatory at the age of nine. His most famous opera, *Carmen*, received much criticism from critics and the public, although Bizet was paid very well for the work. Despite this cold reception of *Carmen*, the opera company kept it in its repertoire, and the work soon became a great success all over the world. This theme is one of the opera's most famous melodies.

Toreador Song

from *Carmen*

Georges Bizet (1838–1875)
Arr. Willard A. Palmer

When listings like this appear in print, one can't help but be amazed by the monumental legacy left behind by composers of the past. Just research the musical library for whatever reason, and this becomes very apparent. Mention putting together a group of spiritual songs, and another treasure box opens. Spiritual songs or hymns can be grouped together in much the same way as Christmas carols. Always include, however, the all-time favorites, "Amazing Grace" and "He's Got the Whole World in His Hands." I can't imagine a spiritual medley without them.

You have much more leeway when creating a medley using popular songs and show tunes. "Mix and match" is the key. Follow this and you'll impress the world. (Refer to Appendix F for playing books and material.)

AN INSTRUMENTAL ARRANGEMENT

I saved the best—the *real* reward—for last. You are now capable of playing something already learned and play it with orchestral accompaniment. Don't be shocked! It's true! I'm referring to the first movement of Beethoven's *Moonlight Sonata* as it appears in its original form in Book Three of *Alfred's Basic Adult Piano Course.*

The concept for an arrangement for the *Moonlight Sonata* came to me while listening to the orchestral part of Tschaikowsky's *Piano Concerto No. 1 in B-flat Minor* played by a Juilliard classmate, pianist Van Cliburn. I envisioned the lush harmony of the string section floating over the melody line of the *Moonlight Sonata* with a deep, rich bass pulsating below. The piano composition remained completely untouched. Fortunately, my drummer doubled on vibraphone (a/k/a vibes.) My bassist supplied the depth of tone *below* by bowing his bass. Thus, the vibes and bass became the orchestra I visualized. In actuality, this is more an orchestration than an arrangement. It became one of my most popular arrangements.

Two small, but important points to note regarding the bass: the standard wooden bass is called an *acoustic* bass. When bowed, it's called *arco*. When plucked with the finger, it's called *pizzicato*. Both techniques are used throughout a symphonic score.

Study the chart for vibes and note that the chords are a mixture of the basic triad and its inversions. As learned in theory, a chord is *inverted* when its root is not at the bass. In this case, I used an ample supply of *seventh chords* because it enriched the harmony. In short, use this combination of chords always concentrating on the *top voice line.* Play the chords apart from the arrangement, and you will see how *tight* the line is. Your ear will confirm this immediately.

To play this arrangement, you will need to find a bassist and a vibraphonist. Check out music schools, private teachers, local orchestras, school bands, and of course, the ever reliable word-of-mouth.

Following is a printout of the three instrumental parts making up the arrangement. The circled letters are there to help locate sections for added work during rehearsal.

Sonata quasi una Fantasia.
(MOONLIGHT)
Op. 27, No. 2

To Countess JULIA GUICCIARDI.

L. van BEETHOVEN.

Abbreviations: M. T. signifies Main Theme; S. T., Sub-Theme; Cl. T., Closing Theme; D. G., Development-group; R., Return; Tr., Transition; Md.-Theme; Ep., Episode.

I. Adagio sostenuto. (♩ = 52.)

sempre pp e con sordini.

14.

a) It is evident that the highest part, as the melody, requires a firmer touch than the accompanying triplet-figure; and the first note in the latter must never produce the effect of a doubling of the melody in the lower octave.

b) A more frequent use of the pedal than is marked by the editor, and limited here to the most essential passages, is allowable; it is not advisable, however, to take the original directions *sempre senza sordini* (i. e., without dampers) too literally.

×11617r

a) The player must guard against carrying his hand back with over-anxious haste. For, in any event, a strict pedantic observance of time is out of place in this period, which has rather the character of an improvisation.

a) The notes with a dash above them may properly be dwelt upon in such a way as to give them the effect of suspensions, e. g., [musical example]: in fact, a utilization of the inner parts, in accordance with the laws of euphony and the course of the modulation, is recommended throughout the piece.

There are books on arrangements in a graded series written by the experts that takes you through the process step by step. Once you become a proficient pianist and a skilled sight-reader, take a look at these books. One such book is a piano solo series called *The Genius of the Jazz Giants* with arrangements by Earl "Fatha" Hines, "Fats" Waller, George Shearing, Art Tatum, and Teddy Wilson among others. Marian McPartland has a book with arrangements, as does George Gershwin. Gershwin's album contains eighteen song hits for piano called *Gershwin at the Keyboard.* America's foremost composer/arranger/conductor, Nelson Riddle, is, without a doubt, one of the all-time prodigies. His book, *The Definitive Study of Arranging,* should be in every musician's library.

You may find yourself developing such a proficiency that you're no longer content to keep your music in the privacy of your own home. You may want to "take your act on the road." That, and numerous other surprising performance opportunities, will be the subject of the final chapter of this book.

8

Playing Possibilities: Volunteer–Professional–Teacher

Do you envision yourself the recipient of an award when you sit and watch pop artists like Billy Joel and Elton John accept yet another award? What about concert artists like Yevgeny Kissin and Midori, who constantly dazzle audiences with their virtuosity and technique?

As a late starter, you might not end up on the stage of Carnegie Hall or as a new recording artist at RCA or Deutsche-Grammaphon. It's also highly unlikely that you'll find yourself sitting on awards night in an audience of celebrities panting as the narrator opens the envelope and calls out your name. Yet, on the other hand, who knows? Don't give up that dream and don't rule anything out! There is no reason why you should keep your aptitude a secret. The good news is that there is a whole range of performance opportunities out there from volunteering to teaching that can be immensely rewarding. What better way is there to get going than by starting with volunteer work?

NURSING AND ADULT HOMES

Earlier, I mentioned how rewarding my work as a volunteer in a nursing home was. To watch patients respond to music and practically "heal" before my eyes was magical. Believe me when I tell you there's no audience more appreciative and attentive than those cooped up in nursing and adult homes. And they *love* music, especially songs they grew up with from the 1920s and 1930s. There is an anthology of playing books recommended for this specific use under the heading *E Z Play Today Series* (see Appendix F). The first listing, *The Decade Series,* is ideal because it covers songs from the 1920s through the 1960s and comes in large print with chords and lyrics (fake book style). Continue down that page and songs by American song legends Cole Porter, Irving Berlin, George Gershwin, Rodgers and Hart, Rodgers and Hammerstein, and Lerner and Lowe abound.

Further scanning will unveil another series not to be overlooked. It's the *Mostly Classical Music* collection—an excellent assortment of music including well-known compositions by Tschaikowsky, Chopin, and Mozart to ragtime, boogie woogie, and Christmas songs. Among the old songs most requested are tunes already known and/or played—"Let Me Call You Sweetheart," "Apple Blossom Time," "Girl of My Dreams," "Till We Meet Again," "I'm a Yankee Doodle Dandy," "Now Is the Hour," "My Wild Irish Rose," and "God Bless America" being typical examples.

If you are retired, volunteering is a nifty way to fill in the gap now that you have a less demanding schedule to keep. Besides having fun and giving much-needed joy to shut-ins and others less fortunate, you get to know the staff and administration. Who knows what budding friendships may ensue.

If your goal is to become a jazz or concert artist, consider appearing in recitals at these facilities either with your peers or alone. You have the perfect audience and ambience. Many trained but unseasoned performers, both artistic and comedic, have been known to try out new material before a pending recital or professional engagement at a home. What better way to experiment with tempo, dynamics and interpretation if an artist, and new routines and jokes if a comedian. You not only give pleasure to grateful listeners, but hone-in on your skills.

For nursing and adult homes, stick to music of their generation with megadoses of patriotic songs. Remember, many were in the armed forces and still retain that pride and patriotism. Also, minds tend to wander if tunes are not familiar. Have a program outlined, but let them run the show. Get residents involved with singing and physical motion such as hand-clapping and foot-tapping. As enthusiasm gains momentum, requests come from all corners of the room, so be prepared. Any song request you can't fulfill, try to learn for the next session. You will gain a devoted follower besides adding to your repertoire.

Hospitals and hospices tend to care for people of all ages, and these patients need cheering up just as much as the nursing-home group. Medical facilities include hospitals and AIDS hospices ministering to younger patients more in tune with what's happening today. While music played in nursing homes is acceptable, it has its limitations and should be expanded to include current material. Update the repertoire with hit tunes by popular artists like Bette Midler and Celine Dion. Their respective hits, "Wind Beneath My Wings" and "My Heart Will Go On" from *Titanic,* continue to top the charts. Broadway musicals with gems like "Memory" from *Cats* and "Send in the Clowns" from *A Little Night Music* have become standards. Although the scores from *Phantom of the Opera* and *Les Miserables* may be irrelevant to nursing-home residents, they catch the ear of the more youthful listener. On the other hand, revivals of Broadway classics like *Annie Get Your Gun, Oklahoma, On the Town,* and *Music Man* are all but unknown to the younger generation, yet senior citizens thrive on them. It's the same with classical music and jazz. Each category has its own distinct, loyal following. While music itself is universally loved and regarded, we tend to go our own favorite way. Therefore, judge your audience and then proceed.

In general, patients of all ages confined either permanently or temporarily need to be encouraged and inspired as much as possible. Music, being the great motivator and communicator, plays a major role in achieving this. By mixing your program with solo piano, sing-a-long sessions, and audience participation, you're doing a wondrous deed not only for the less fortunate, but for yourself.

ELECTRIC KEYBOARDS IN INSTITUTIONS

With musical knowledge now under your belt and new songs steadily adding to your repertoire, wouldn't it be a feather in your cap to *teach* some of the infirm how to play? Consider using this as an alternative to playing for recreational sessions. These sessions are pre-arranged, and once you commit, you are expected to adhere to the schedule. With individual teaching, you can come and go as you please and set your own schedule. I visited a friend's mother in a nursing home and heard sounds coming from the room across the hall. It turned out to be a resident playing the electronic keyboard. She played piano all of her life, so having a keyboard in her room was a *must.* But there are those who have always longed to play, and *you* can help make that dream come true. Remember, Yankee legend Yogi Berra said, "It ain't over til it's over." In this case, even a Casio with a reduced keyboard and buttons for chords is fine. The purpose is to fill those idle hours and finally satisfy that longing. What it does for the human spirit is beyond measure.

If the nursing home doesn't already have keyboards in stock, speak to administration about purchasing a few. I am looking at an ad right now listing one for $9.99. They can be purchased in any electronic, department or discount store. There is no maintenance involved, and eventually they'll be passed along to other residents. Another thought is to contact a local entrepreneur about making a donation toward the purchase. Don't forget to approach family members and friends as they stop by to visit. It might not have crossed their minds to give a keyboard at holiday time.

When teaching a resident, find out their favorite songs and proceed to teach those first. *The Decade Series,* mentioned earlier, is the perfect book and the only one they'll need. It covers all the songs they already know and is in large print with chords and lyrics. Insist they do *not* bring their keyboard to the recreational session! Can you imagine trying to restore order with all that clamor going on?

TEACHING CHILDREN

If you love children as I do, there is nothing more enchanting and motivating than little voices emanating from children's wards and day-care centers singing nursery rhymes at the top of their lungs. There is no shortage of repertory for children either (see Appendix F). In the collection, *Nursery Rhymes for All Keyboards,* songs every child learns early on, like "A-Tisket, A-Tasket," "Mary Had a Little Lamb," and "Twinkle, Twinkle Little Star" are included.

For fun, make a game out of "rounds." A *round* is a type of composition in which the different participants begin the same melody one after another at regular intervals. It is also referred to as a "canon" in classical music. Two of the most famous rounds are "Row, Row, Row Your Boat" and "Frère Jacques." Try to get the children to listen and join in at the designated time. Teach them "Eensy Weensy Spider" and watch their eyes focus intently on the finger work mimicking a crawling spider. Play songs with a strong beat, like "The Marines' Hymn" and "God Bless America," as they march around the room marking time. They are not only being taught how to synchronize coordination

and beat-keeping, they are learning our country's favorite patriotic songs, too. Subconsciously, these tiny ears are absorbing
harmony and intervals that will come into play at a later age.

Break it up with "time out." Remember, children tend to be
hyperactive and have short attention spans. Videos abound with
favorite cartoons, so play these while you take a much-needed
reprise. Learn the cartoon theme songs—you will probably be
asked to play them. They can be found almost anywhere children's items are sold—supermarkets, toy stores, department
and book stores and, of course, music stores. As with entertain-
ing the elderly, let *them* run the show. They already do, whether
we know it or not. Mix singing with games, videos, and the reading of stories and fairy tales, and you'll find all the money in the
world cannot replace the love and affection that will pour your
way.

PLAYING IN PUBLIC

If you are doing volunteer work at this point and have enough
repertoire under your belt, transfer this expertise to your social
life. Your "Hey, gang—look what I learned!" will set your social
calendar afire. All you have to do is play the music already
learned and add to it (see Appendix F). *Movie Musical
Memories* in the *E Z Play Today Series* includes standard songs
ideal for any party. Learn how to play "Happy Birthday" and
"The Anniversary Song," and the piano is yours for the asking.
Scan the rest of the anthology for whatever else is needed.
Combine these with fake books and you have a comprehensive
library of standard songs. You'll find that as you repeat certain
tunes, you're automatically memorizing them through the process of repetition. Eventually, you won't have to cart around
your music. It would be a smart move to memorize the lyrics.
It's a plus when it comes to keeping the momentum afloat.

Party-goers will lip-read you like a teleprompter when they don't know all the lyrics themselves.

If you attempted to transpose simple songs at home and feel comfortable with it, this is as good a time as any to "break the ice." Chances are the party is well under way and you already scored high points. Slip in well-worn evergreens like "My Wild Irish Rose" and "When Irish Eyes Are Smiling"—perfect party songs. The good news is they have just *four* chord changes. The *best* news is, if you slip up, zealous voices will drown you out.

Two tips to pass along at this point! Most songs are written in keys too high for the average voice, and the mature voice slowly drops in pitch as we age (an important point to remember when playing for senior citizens). Experience has shown that a comfortable singing key for the average voice is anywhere from a third to a fifth *below* the original—e.g., if the original is in the key of C, a *third* below is *A* or *A-flat,* a *fourth* below is *G,* a *fifth* below is *F.* The normal singing range is approximately an octave and a half, so if the song extends beyond, the barometer to follow is: the lower, the better. Jot down the transposition key on the song sheet and make notes of chords that "hang you up." With repetition, you'll start incorporating more intricate songs.

Now that you're "on a roll," try playing for ceremonies and functions at the local civic clubs in your area. If you are retired or about to retire, what a golden opportunity to make new friends and enjoy leisure time. Playing at such functions is the same as playing for any audience. Same material—different people.

PLAYING IN CHURCH

Years ago, the opportunity to become a church musician would have been out of the question for any instrumentalist except an organist. Church and organ went together like fish and chips. Today, the piano is as acceptable in churches as guitar and brass ensembles with drums. Actually, I started to play in church at the age of five. The instrument was an electrified piano without foot pedals and not an organ (whose pedals I could not have reached). A few years later, I got paid to play at weddings and funerals.

There are only a few select songs to play at these occasions. Music stores sell books for special events like weddings that include the traditional "Bridal Chorus" from Wagner's *Lohengrin* and "Wedding March" from Mendelssohn's *Midsummer Night's Dream* plus "The Lord's Prayer" and both Schubert's and Gounod's "Ave Maria." If a vocalist is engaged to sing, it's simply a matter of being the accompanist and not the soloist. Contact your local church and temple for more specific information. They should also be able to supply the music played at funerals.

SUBSTITUTE MUSICIAN

If you can play "Silent Night," you can play *any* hymn. The most famous Christmas carol of all time is written around *three* chords. Take your church hymnal home, play the hymns you know, and you will find this to be so with other hymns. Learn them and perhaps suggest becoming the substitute musician for the church choir. Who knows? The regular musician might move or retire and *there you are!*

Today, opportunities once closed to the budding musician are popping up all over the place. There is *no* reason, at this point, why you can't take advantage of this and start receiving compensation! You've put in the practice time, you learned the tunes, and you are now ready to reap the rewards. If you have gotten your feet wet doing volunteer work and playing at parties and houses of worship, more opportunities abound. Don't blink your eyes when I mention institutions like jails, banks and department stores. Digital pianos have opened the doors for background music and recreational activity never thought of before.

Technology made all this possible. Prior to the breakthrough, an employer had the responsibility of providing a piano. No more! Today, the musician can wheel in the keyboard and speakers, set himself up, and play an instrument familiar to him. No more shuddering at the possibility of an out-of-tune piano.

Here is a list of some of those opportunities followed by a brief description and source of contact:

- Certain jails have hired and *still* hire music as therapy for inmates. For the protection of all, the premises are carefully monitored and screened for safety. Information about agencies that send units and soloists to entertain in these facilities can be obtained by contacting the institution directly. The government issues grants from time to time to pay for live music, and most often transportation is provided.
- Occasionally you see a pianist playing in a bank lobby for an hour or two a day. The older, stately facilities are more conducive to such a setting. The piano is cordoned off from the business area but remains within sight. Approach management and give them food for thought. You already know what to play. If agreed upon, whatever the stipend is that's offered, it's a plus for you. The added touch is soothing to the harried customer, and this is a clever format, on the part of the bank, to enhance business.

  It probably never crossed your mind that jails and banks would employ musicians. And it doesn't stop there! When I first encountered a pianist playing a grand piano in the upscale department store, Nordstrom, in Seattle, Washington, I was pleasantly surprised. Live music is now sprouting up in the most unexpected places, such as the lounging areas of malls and museums as well as chic boutiques along Rodeo Drive in Beverly Hills, California, and Worth Avenue in Palm Beach, Florida. At Christmas time, many corporations and hotels throughout the world feature local choirs singing seasonal songs in their lobbies. How long does it take to learn these traditional songs anyway? They've been a part of our lives since childhood. Besides, an accompanist is needed. If a piano is not on the premises, it can easily be arranged.

- Selling pianos and keyboards in a music store is another avenue to explore. Certainly an excellent way to pull in money in commissions. Many musicians supplement their incomes this way. Whether you contemplate a part-time or a full-time position, know beforehand it's not what it seems to be. Proficiency at the piano is the *least* of it. What gets you the job is your *knowledge* of the instruments being sold. With acoustic pianos, a bit of history and an explanation of the makes, models and structure is pertinent. This was addressed in an earlier chapter.

  With digital keyboards, it's a whole new ballgame. More elaborate instruments arrive at the stores periodically and the salesperson must keep up-to-date. Study the brochures, have hands-on experience with the new merchandise before approaching a customer, and you're ahead of the game. We know the keyboard itself doesn't change—it's the paraphernalia surrounding it. Technology never ceases to amaze!

  You might be asked to play, but chances are the potential buyer has some knowledge of the keyboard and is eager to play it himself. His decision will be based on how the instrument responds to him and not on how it sounds to others. If you're asked to play, it's solely for the benefit of the customer who just wants to check the resonance, depth of tone, clarity, etc. Selling is a good way to supplement income while leaning.

- Being an accompanist for a vocalist, instrumentalist or group can be a most satisfying experience. However, it does require sight-reading skills and an ability to follow. These abilities instinctively fine-tune your abilities as you rehearse.

  As the "supporter," it is to your advantage to become familiar with the lyrics. This gives you freedom to phrase with the soloist and adapt to any fluctuations in tempo. Remain the back-up and don't overpower! Schools now offer courses in accompaniment to pianists because it's become so popular and lucrative. When did you last hear a soloist perform a cappella? The opportunities abound for both the professional and the volunteer—playing for auditions, recitals, competitions, coaching, rehearsals (dance/instrumental/vocal), choirs, a chorus—quite an impressive list. Practice sight-reading diligently and make the right contacts when you feel ready.

Just a bit of advice to singers on why it's to your advantage to learn the piano. First of all, the criterion is not to play well. Remember, the piano is not your forte. The principle reason is to be able to help yourself when an accompanist isn't around. You won't need assistance when you can limber up and learn a new song or aria on your own. Playing along as you vocalize will strengthen your sense of pitch. Your scales and exercises will take on a new freedom and flexibility because of the added support. This knowledge will also open the door to better communication with instrumental musicians. The best part is that it cuts the expense of having an accompanist around at all times. Think about it.

SUPPLEMENTING YOUR INCOME

When you started taking piano lessons, did it ever occur to you that someday you might pass along your acquired knowledge to others? Frequently, friends and peers relate stories of going back to school to "take a course." It's either something they've always *wanted* to do or something they *need* to do to supplement their income. Frequently, the media dispatches information about how to augment one's income. Today, it's common to have both spouses working for that very reason. Once a family is on the way, it's stressful for the mother to continue working and care for the family/home and tend to chores. She eventually winds up making a decision either to continue to forfeit her paycheck to day care or throw in the "work" towel.

That's where teaching comes into play. A mother can supplement the family income by *teaching* piano. If she's played since childhood or took lessons later in life, arrangements can be made to give lessons to children at home and in the neighborhood. It's limiting at first while the family is young, but as responsibilities lift and more free time opens up, a full-time teaching career may be in the making.

If teaching piano was never intended to be a career and you are contemplating the possibility, take the necessary courses to upgrade your skills and become acquainted with the up-to-date teaching material. The courses recommended for adults are also written for children (see Appendix D). As a matter of fact, there appears to be more on the market for children than adults.

At this point, there is no reason why you can't move forward to include adults as well as children. You're aware of the instruction and playing material at hand, and you know to what extent you are qualified. Be honest with yourself and your students. If you cannot take them beyond a certain point, make sources available so they can continue. I wish my instructors were more forthright about their limitations, so take heed. Unfortunately, the world is saturated with incompetency in every field. Don't add to it.

It sounds as though I excluded fathers from the teaching scene. Not so. Most often, fathers are the head of the household, and being the breadwinner leaves little time for teaching. Once the children leave the nest, restrictions and commitments ease, giving more time to teach.

PLAYING PIANO DUETS

Playing piano duets is great fun for children and adults. Children are especially excited by this "new game" and need little or no enticement. Whether the combination is adult-with-adult or child-with-adult, both are about to hit a barrier. That barrier is *less* freedom and *more* discipline. Once the meter is established, both participants are expected to adhere to tempo. There is a natural tendency to rush because both players are anxious. That's where discipline comes in. Use a metronome if necessary. The anxiety will subside as the newness wears off and each partner then becomes more relaxed. Can you imagine a child's ego trip when playing duets with a parent? Suddenly he/she becomes your peer and wants to take over.

Piano duets are written for both one piano—four hands, and two pianos—four hands (see Appendix E). Literature for two pianos was never as popular as for one piano because most households only had one piano. Now with digital keyboards, things have changed. Playing duets also prepares a person for ensemble and chamber work. With three or more people playing together, it's imperative to listen to each other to achieve that cohesive sound—the key component in orchestral playing. The conductor's job is to "fuse" the instrumental sounds into an artistic blend in order to interpret the musical score. He will only achieve this if he has the undivided attention of each player.

Wouldn't it be nice if you lived in a community that had its own civic orchestra? What a pleasurable experience to play with other instrumentalists who enjoy music as much as you. No, it's not the New York Philharmonic, but it's just as exciting. Who would have thought when you first started to learn the piano that you'd end up being a symphonic player! The opportunities are there and waiting to be filled. You've worked hard and are now ready to reap the rewards. Go for it and good luck!

APPENDICES

APPENDIX A:
Music Schools in the United States

ARIZONA

Arizona State University College of Fine Arts, School of Music
Tempe, Arizona 85287-0405
Telephone: 1-602-965-3371
Fax: 1-602-965-2659

CALIFORNIA

University of California, Los Angeles School of the Arts,
Department of Music
1147 Murphy Hill
Los Angeles, California 90024
Telephone: 1-310-825-3101
Fax: 1-310-825-8099

University of Southern California, School of Music
Los Angeles, California 90089-0851
Telephone: 1-800-872-2213 and 1-213-743-2741
Fax: 1-213-740-3217

University of California, Santa Barbara, College of Letters
and Sciences, Department of Music
1210 Cheadle Hall
Santa Barbara, California 93106
Telephone: 1-805-893-2881
Fax: 1-805-893-8779

COLORADO

University of Colorado at Boulder, College of Music
Box 301
Boulder, Colorado 80309
Telephone: 1-303-492-6352
Fax: 1-303-492-5619

CONNECTICUT

Yale University, School of Music
New Haven, Connecticut 06520
Telephone: 1-203-432-4155
Fax: 1-203-432-7542

University of Hartford, Hartt School of Music
200 Bloomfield Avenue
West Hartford, Connecticut 06117
Telephone: 1-203-768-4465
Fax: 1-203-768-4441

ILLINOIS

Northern Illinois University College of Visual and
Performing Arts, School of Music
De Kalb, Illinois 60115-2857
Telephone: 1-815-753-0446
Fax: 1-815-753-1783

Northwestern University School of Music
71 Elgin Road
Evanston, Illinois 60208-1200
Telephone: 1-708-491-3141
Fax: 1-708-491-5260

University of Illinois at Urbana School of Music
1114 W. Nevada St.
Urbana, Illinois 61801
Telephone: 1-217-244-0551
Fax: 1-217-244-4585

INDIANA

University School of Music
Bloomington, Indiana 47405
Telephone: 1-812-855-7998
Fax: 1-812-855-4936

IOWA

University of Northern Iowa School of Music
120 Gilchrist
Cedar Falls, Iowa 50614-0018
Telephone: 1-319-273-2281
Fax: 1-319-273-2888

MARYLAND

The Peabody Conservatory of Music
1 East Mount Vernon Ave.
Baltimore, MD 21202-2397
Telephone: 1-410-695-8110
Fax: 1-410-659-8102

University of Maryland College Park, Department of Music
College Park, Maryland 20742
Telephone: 1-301-314-8385

MICHIGAN

University of Michigan, School of Music
1100 Bapes Dr.
Ann Arbor, Michigan 48109-2085
Telephone: 1-734-764-0583

Michigan State University School of Music
103 Music Building
East Lansing, Michigan 48824
Telephone: 1-517-355-2140
Fax: 1-517-336-2880

MISSOURI

University of Missouri—Columbia, Department of Music,
School of Fine Arts
Columbia, Missouri 65211
Telephone: 1-314-882-2456
Fax: 1-314-882-7887

University of Missouri—Kansas City, Conservatory of Music
5100 Rockhill Rd.
Kansas City, Missouri 64110
Telephone: 1-816-235-1136
Fax: 1-816-235-5191

NEW JERSEY

Rutgers University—New Brunswick, Mason Gross School
of the Arts, Music Department
Box 270
New Brunswick, New Jersey 08903
Telephone: 1-908-932-9302
Fax: 1-908-932-1517

NEW YORK

The Juilliard School
60 Lincoln Center Plaza
New York, New York 10023
Telephone: 1-212-799-5000 ext. 223
Fax: 1-212-724-0263

Manhattan School of Music
120 Claremont Avenue
New York, New York 10027-4698
Telephone: 1-212-749-3025
Fax: 1-212-749-5471

Mannes College of Music
150 W. 85th Street
New York, New York 10024
Telephone: 1-212-580-0210 ext. 4647

State University of New York at Stony Brook,
Department of Music
Stony Brook, New York 11794-5475
Telephone: 1-631-632-7330
Fax: 1-631-632-6252

University of Rochester, Eastman School of Music
26 Gibbs Street
Rochester, New York 14604
Telephone: 1-716-274-1060
Fax: 1-716-263-2807

OHIO

University of Cincinnati, College Conservatory of Music
Cincinnati, Ohio 45221-0003
Telephone: 1-513-556-5462
Fax: 1-513-556-1028

The Cleveland Institute of Music
11021 East Boulevard
Cleveland, Ohio 44106
Telephone: 1-216-795-3107
Fax: 1-216-791-1530

PENNSYLVANIA

The Curtis Institute of Music
1726 Locust Street
Philadelphia, Pennsylvania 19103
Telephone: 1-215-893-5252
Fax: 1-215-893-0194

TEXAS

University of Texas at Austin, Department of Music
Austin, Texas 78712
Telephone: 1-512-471-0504
Fax: 1-512-471-7836

University of North Texas, College of Music
Denton, Texas 76203
Telephone: 1-817-565-2681
Fax: 1-817-565-2141

Rice University, Sheperd School of Music
Box 1892
Houston, Texas 77251
Telephone: 1-713-527-5854
Fax: 1-713-285-5317

WASHINGTON

University of Washington, School of Music
Seattle, Washington 98195
Telephone: 1-206-543-9686
Fax: 1-206-543-8798

WASHINGTON, DC

Catholic University of America, The Benjamin T. Rome
School of Music
620 Michigan Avenue
Washington, DC 20064
Telephone: 1-202-319-5305 and 1-800-673-2772
Fax: 1-202-319-5199

WISCONSIN

University of Wisconsin—Madison, School of Music
433 N. Murray St.
Madison, Wisconsin 53706
Telephone: 1-608-263-5016
Fax: 1-608-262-8876

APPENDIX B:
Adult Courses in New York City

Turtle Bay Music School—244 E. 52nd St.—Telephone: 1-212-753-8811

Juilliard School–Lincoln Center—Telephone: 1-212-799-5000

Mannes College of Music—150 W. 85th St.—Telephone: 1-212-580-0210

Manhattan School of Music—120 Claremont Ave.—Telephone: 1-212-749-2802

Third Street Music School Settlement—235 E. 11th St.—Telephone: 1-212-777-3240

92nd Street School of Music—1395 Lexington Ave.—Telephone: 1-212-415-5580

Gramercy Park School of Music—9 E. 36th St.—Telephone: 1-212-683-8937

Academy of Musical Art—Emilia Del Terzo—Carnegie Hall, 57th St. and Seventh Ave.—Telephone: 1-212-246-3154

Diller-Quaile School of Music—24 E. 95th St.—Telephone: 1-212-369-1484

Dalcroze School of Music—161 E. 73rd St.—Telephone: 1-212-879-0316

APPENDIX C:
Teaching Associations in the United States

The National Association of Music Teachers
617 Vine Street, Suite 1432
Cincinnati, Ohio 45202

The National Guild of Piano Teachers
Box 1807
Austin, Texas 78767
Telephone 1-512-478-5775
Publishes "Piano Guild Notes"

The Official Journal of Music Teachers National Association
408 Carew Tower, 441 Vine Street, Suite 505
Cincinnati, Ohio 45202-2814

"The Most Wanted Teachers in the U.S.A." by Benjamin Saver.
Publisher: X in Hua Ma in Los Angeles, California

APPENDIX D:
Piano Courses

Michael Aaron: Adult Piano Course—two books. Includes dictionary of musical terms, arpeggios, triads, technique (Hanon), theory, scales, chords, and song material.

Kenneth Baker: The Complete Piano Player—an omnibus edition published by Amsco in a 6-book series. A piano course based on pop songs and light classics. Easy to follow for progression into advanced playing. For home use or classroom study.

Mel Bay Publications, Inc.: You Can Teach Yourself Piano. Publisher: Mel Bay Publications, Inc., #4 Industrial Dr., Pacific, Missouri 63099-0066. Telephone: 1-800-863-5229

John Brimhall: Young Adult Piano Course and *Theory Notebook*— 4-book series, recognizable songs. Other Brimhall books are *Big Tri-Chord Piano Book, The Best of Seven in One, Adult Piano Course.* Contains numerous arrangements of current pop hits. He has fakebook style collections as well.

Leila Fletcher: The Leila Fletcher Adult Piano Course, designed to enjoy while learning. Publisher: The Boston Music Co., 172 Fremont St., Boston, MA 02111

Hershal Pyle: The University Piano Series for Adult Students. 2-book series, Campus Publications, Bradenton, Florida

Ada Richter: The Ada Richter Piano Course for the older student. Includes recognized songs plus theory, technique, time and rhythm, pedal, dictionary of terms and signs. Publisher: Warner Brothers Publications, Inc., 15800 N.W. 48th Ave., Miami, Florida 33014

John Thompson: John Thompson's Adult Piano Book, I and II. Contains pieces from classic composers Brahms, Wagner, Bach, Mozart, Liszt, Chopin, etc.—*John Thompson's Adult Preparatory Piano Book* to be used in conjunction with teacher. Publisher: The Willis Music Co., Florence, Kentucky 41022

APPENDIX E:
How-To Piano Books

Piano Playing contains questions about the piano that are answered by legendary pianist, Josef Hofmann. It is published by Dover.

Teach Yourself the Piano by King Palmer, an associate of the Royal Academy of Music, discusses the process of learning the piano.

How to Play Piano by Roger Evans, published by St. Martin's Press, talks about how to play and read sheet music. It has information about the instrument itself such as how to buy, move, tune, and place a piano.

How to Play Keyboards by Roger Evans, published by St. Martin's Press, talks about how modern technology produces unique sounds and rhythms electronically. It addresses the sliding buttons that change tempo, rhythm, and volume, the controls, headphones, start/stop buttons and explains how to get various instrumental effects like the organ, strings, and brass. It's quite informative.

APPENDIX F:
Playing Books and Series

E Z PLAY TODAY SERIES: published by Hal Leonard—comes in large print with chords and lyrics, fake book style. Excellent!

The Decade Series—songs of the 20s through 60s.

Broadway Musicals—show-by-show book for piano, organ, and electronic keyboards. Runs chronologically from 1891 through today. Contains songs by Porter, Berlin, Gershwin, Rodgers and Hart, Rodgers and Hammerstein, Lerner and Lowe, etc.

"Movie Musical Memories"—contains torch songs through arias. Examples include "The Anniversary Song," "Over the Rainbow," "Singing in the Rain," etc.

"One for My Lady"—'Fifty Women Made Famous in Song,' based on female names.

"It's Gospel"—featuring "Amazing Grace" and "I Believe."

"Jazz Standards"—contains "April in Paris," "Body and Soul," "Out of Nowhere," songs of Duke Ellington like "Satin Doll," "Don't Get Around Much Anymore," "It Don't Mean a Thing If It Ain't Got That Swing."

"The Rodgers and Hammerstein Song Book"—contains songs from *Carousel, South Pacific, Oklahoma, The King and I, The Sound of Music.*

THE PIANO CONCEPTS SERIES: (good)—"Great Themes from TV and Movies" for easy to intermediate, arranged by Jan Thomas. Songs include "Tara's Theme" from *Gone With the Wind,* "Chariots of Fire," "Anything Goes," "The Way We Were," "Nadia's Theme" from *The Young and the Restless,* "Speak Softly Love" from *The Godfather,* "A Time for Us" from *Romeo And Juliet.*

MOSTLY CLASSICAL MUSIC:
An *excellent* series in full sheet music form from easy to intermediate. Arranger: Barry Todd Publisher: Music Sales Limited,

Newmarket Road, Bury St. Edmunds, Suffolk IP3334B, England. Telephone: 0284-702600. Fax: 0284-768301.

It's Easy to Play Tschaikowsky

It's Easy to Play Strauss

It's Easy to Play Ragtime

It's Easy to Play Bach

It's Easy to Play Ballads—Beatles, Blues, Beethoven, Boogie Woogie, Children's Songs, Chopin, Mozart, Gershwin, Christmas Songs, songs from the 20s through the 80s

Beethoven—I Can Play That

Bach—I Can Play That

Handel—I Can Play That

For intermediate level, arranged by Stephen Duro with chord symbols. Wise Publications, Located at Barnes & Noble.

One Hundred Classical Melodies—contains only music, no chords; memorable themes and immortal classics. Included are "Romeo and Juliet Love Theme," "Rachmaninoff Piano Concerto #2 Theme," "Theme from Carmen," "Tschaikowsky Piano Concerto #1 Theme," "Merry Widow Waltz," "Blue Danube," "Für Elise," "Pavane for a Dead Princess," "Sleeping Beauty Waltz," "Claire de Lune," "Ode to Joy" (Beethoven's 9th Symphony), "Musetta's Waltz" from Puccini's *La Boheme*. Located at Barnes & Noble.

The Library of Easy Classics—original form—published by Amsco

The Library of Easy Ragtime And Blues

The Library of Easy Piano Classics

Favorite Classical Melodies—for easy piano—published by Ekay Music Inc., 223 Katonah Avenue, Katonah, New York 10536

Music For Millions Series—Play Piano with Three Chords—*excellent.* Consolidated Music Publishers

Big Note Piano—"Timeless Standards"—large print

Hooked on Easy Piano Classics Three—arranged and edited by Ralph Cruickshank

Assorted Recommendations:

CHILDREN

Nursery Rhymes for All Keyboards—Published by Wise Publications. Music plus chord symbols; songs included are: "A-Tisket, A-Tasket," "Mary Had a Little Lamb," "Pat-a-Cake," "Row, Row, Row Your Boat," "Twinkle, Twinkle Little Star," "Skip to My Lou," "Eensy Weensy Spider," "Frère Jacques," "London Bridge," "Little Jack Horner," "Little Miss Muffet"

DUETS

Duet Favorites—Jane Bastien. Three levels, one piano—four hands (good)

Pop Standards for Two Pianos

The Best of Ferrante and Teicher's Piano Duets" (advanced)

EXERCISES

Dozen a Day—exercise series

The School of Octave Playing for the Piano—Kullah

C.L. Hanon—The Virtuose Pianist—exercises, scales, chromatic scales, arpeggios, for strength, flexibility, independence, evenness. Published by Carl Fischer.

Exercise books: Czerny, Clementi, Dohnanyi

David Hirschberg: Technic for Adults (Czerny)—all exercises

JAZZ

Rick Wald's Guide to Creative Jazz Improvisation

Mainstreams in Music by Carol and Walter Noona, published by Heritage Music Press, a 3-book series called *The Improviser* designed to teach basic jazz, improvisation, how to supply bass and fill-ins. Considered one of the best organized and instructive in jazz

RAGTIME

Scott Joplin: "The Entertainer" and "Maple Leaf Rag"

David Carr Glover published by Belwin-Mills—various styles such as boogie woogie, blues, rag

OPERA

It's Easy to Play Opera—simplified arrangements of operatic melodies arranged by Frank Booth

BIG BAND

The Best of Sweet and Simple and *The Big Band Hits*—published by Creative Concepts Publishing Co. This is for all electronic keyboards

COUNTRY

Easy Piano: Today's Country Hits, edited by Milton Okun

TAPES FOR EDUCATION

EDUCO has tapes for teaching the beginning student (Heritage)

APPENDIX G:
Music Stores in New York City and Pennsylvania

Joseph Patelson Music House, Ltd. at 160 West 56th St., New York, NY 10019. Telephone: 1-212-582-5840 or 1-800-733-1474 Fax: 212-246-5633. Their library is very extensive in the teaching and classical field. Music schools like Juilliard recommend Patelson Ltd. highly. To this day, it stands in the same landmark building erected in 1879.

Colony Record and Tape Center at 1619 Broadway, New York, NY 10019. Telephone: 1-212-265-2050 or 265-1260. Fax: 212-956-6009. E-mail: thecolony1@aol.com They cater largely to the popular music trade and have a huge section of teaching books and fake books. Racks of *how-to* and *study* books covering ear-training, breaks, fill-ins, improvisation, modern styles, harmonic construction, introductions and endings. Targets persons of varying abilities. Much of this material is also available in audio and video.

Sam Ash Music Store at 160 West 48th Street, New York, NY 10036. Telephone: 1-212-719-2299 or 1-212-398-6074. Fax: 212-302-1388. For their quick-ship number, call 1-800-4-SAM ASH. They cover all the above material and excel in teaching literature and self-teaching videos.

In Pennsylvania: Theodore Presser Publishing Co. at 1 Presser Place, Bryn Mawr, PA 19010. Telephone: 1-610-525-3636. The telephone number of Presser's retail store in the same building is: 1-610-527-4242. Another branch is located at 1718 Chestnut Street in Philadelphia, PA 19103. Telephone: 1-215-568-0964.

APPENDIX H
Piano Disc

Piano Disc, 4111-A North Freeway Blvd., Sacramento, California 95834. Telephone: 1-800-566-DISC or 1-919-567-9999. Fax: 1-916-567-1941. Web site: www.pianodisc.com

APPENDIX I:
Songwriting Books

Beginning Songwriter's Answer Book by Paul Zollo—catalog #10376—answers questions most asked by beginning songwriters.

Creating Melodies by Dick Weissman—catalog #10400—tells how to create melodies from love ballads to commercial jingles.

Successful Lyric Writing: A Step-by Step Course and Workbook by Sheila Davis—catalog #10015—is a hands-on course in writing.

The Craft of Lyric Writing by Sheila Davis—catalog #1148—is a complete guide on writing for words and to music.

The Songwriter's Idea Book by Sheila Davis—catalog #10320—illustrates ways to spark your personal creativity.

Writing Better Lyrics by Pat Pattison—catalog #10453—uses seventeen songs to show what makes them so extraordinary.

88 Song Writing Wrongs and How to Right Them by Pat and Pete Luboff.

Songwriting and the Creative Process by Steve Gillette is published by Sing-Out Corporation. It has suggestions and starting points for songwriters.

(The above books are published by Writer's Digest Books, 1507 Dana Avenue, Cincinnati, Ohio 45207. Tel:1-800-289-0963.)

Song Writing by Stephen Citron discusses lyrics, music, rhyme, rhythm, notation, concept, form, and style. Published by Proscenium Publishers, Inc., 118 East 30th Street, New York, New York 10016. Tel: 1-212-532-5525.

APPENDIX J:
Songwriter's Market Guide

The Songwriter's Market Guide to Song and Demo Submission Formats from the editors of *Songwriter's Market.* It advises on query letters, demo presentation and the industry in general.

Hot Tips for the Home Recording Studios by Hank Linderman offers suggestions on recording your own professional demo.

APPENDIX K:
Popular Piano-Playing Books

Beginner's Guide to Popular Piano Playing

Chord Construction and Hints for Popular Piano Playing

Modern Styles and Harmonic Construction for Popular Piano Playing

Marvin Kahn's Breaks, Fillers, Endings and Introductions for Popular Piano

(Published by Warner Brothers Publications, 15800 N.W. 48th Avenue, Miami, Florida 33014. Tel. 1-800-327-7643 or 1-305-620-1500.

APPENDIX L:
Book of Modulation

Mel Bay's Complete Book of Modulation for the Pianist by Gail Smith. Contact Mel Bay Publishers, Inc., 4 Industrial Dr., Pacific, Missouri 63099-0066. Telephone: 1-800-863-5229.